"One of the most fascinating Christian biographies I have ever read. Difficult to put down. A well-written testimony to the grace of God in the life of one of His great pioneers. This book cannot help but challenge all who read it to greater faith in a great God."

Charles C. Ryrie, Ph.D.
Dean of Doctoral Studies and
Professor of Systematic Theology
Dallas Theological Seminary

"Since those earliest days of *Child Evangelism* magazine, in which I had the privilege to have a part, the work has grown so fantastically that it is almost hard to believe. And yet I suspect that there is very, very much more ahead. I am so happy that an account of this great work of God and its human father is finally available to all of us. Many of the details in this book were not known to me till I read them here!"

Kenneth N. Taylor, President
Tyndale House Publishers
Author, Living Letters

"Change demands prior vision. *The Indomitable Mr. O* was avant-garde in the stream of change. But this man knew that, though we may restructure methods, we dare not alter foundations. It is still rock, not sand. Here is a book unique in its counsel for our times."

Ken Anderson
Author, Producer
Ken Anderson Films

"Indomitable he was, the amazing Mr. O! Author Rohrer, in telling the story of J. I. Overholtzer, has given us a blueprint for success in Christian service. Nothing came easy for Mr. O, apparently, and—while he does not stop to preach or moralize —Rohrer drives home again and again the need for stubborn faithfulness in the work of God. This is honest, objective, helpful biography . . . in a way reminiscent of the psychologically oriented life-writing of Andre Maurois on the psychographs of Gamaliel Bradford."

Larry Ward, L.L.D., L.H.D.
Vice President/Overseas Director
World Vision International

The Indomitable Mr. O

The Story of J. Irvin Overholtzer
Founder of the
Child Evangelism Fellowship

By Norman Rohrer

CHILD EVANGELISM FELLOWSHIP PRESS
Warrenton, Missouri

Copyright © 1970 by Child Evangelism Fellowship Inc.

Printed in U.S.A.

All rights reserved

DEDICATED

To the heirs of his vision

Contents

Preface	9
The Past Is Prologue	11
Over the Hills to Tomorrow	17
Why Not Me?	24
Slamming the Castle Gate	32
Liberation!	39
Beards, Bonnets and an Empty Soul	45
Prisoner of Law	49
Assurance on a Stepladder	56
Here I Stand!	61
Knicker and Pigtail Experiment	67
To the Busy Haunts of Men	73
Unfolding Vision	78
Chicago Crucible	84
Trajectory!	93
O is for Organization	100
Man in a Hurry	106
South to the Harvest	114
To the Children of the World	122
The Same in Any Language	129
Grace All the Way	138
As a Tree	142

Preface

Jesse Irvin Overholtzer was the "unobtrusive little farmer" who staked all on the premise — revolutionary in his day — that little children could be taught basic doctrines of the Scriptures and be won for Jesus Christ.

He was unpretentious and unassuming in the pulpit, yet he moved great audiences with his revolutionary message.

He had a weak and faltering voice, yet thousands recognized it as the voice of God drawing them into his knicker and pigtail crusade.

He had neither a degree in theology nor titled position, but he received the support and devoted friendship of such evangelical notables as Harry A. Ironside, Charles G. Trumbull, Paul W. Rood, Walter L. Wilson, M.D., and Henry C. Thiessen.

At sixty years of age, without administrative experience, but with God's enablement, he founded Child Evangelism Fellowship and directed its international operation for fifteen years, to within three years of his death in 1955.

Where might and power failed, the Spirit of God succeeded. Out of the ashes of human weakness came the largest evangelistic outreach to children the world has ever seen.

"Mr. O's" heritage lay deep in the stolid traditions of the Pennsylvania Dutch. Those who understand the meat-and-potatoes approach to life of these stoical Nordics will understand at once Mr. Overholtzer's methodical and unrelieved pace in the execution of the task God gave him to do.

When others asked, "Why?" Mr. O asked, "Why not?" and lived by the motto: "There is no lack with God!"

I am indebted to his widow, Ruth, for cooperating fully in the research . . . to his family . . . to Ruth E. Turnwall, editor and associate of Mr. O's, for her painstaking accumulation of biographical detail . . . to the Child Evangelism Fellowship home office and workers at home and overseas for individual and collective assistance . . . and to my own two little boys who have patiently waited a year and a half to go fishing ". . . until Daddy finishes the book!"

N. R.

The italicized paragraphs and other basic biographical material were taken from J. Irvin Overholtzer's book, A Modern Weeping Prophet, *now out of print.*

The Past Is Prologue

Mid-nineteenth century revival fires were blazing in Scotland when a young Connecticut seminary student entered the country to sit at the feet of the Gamaliels of Edinburgh.

E. Payson Hammond, excited by the fresh winds of spiritual renewal, eagerly took part in speaking missions in Scottish churches.

One day, following a service in the town of Musselburgh, he was out of the church and down the street before he realized he had forgotten his overcoat. Returning to the vestry, he found the door bolted. He rattled the handle impatiently, for he needed his coat against the chilling winter breezes off the Firth of Forth.

Presently the door opened and a little six-year-old girl appeared. Hammond asked for his coat and the little one hurried to get it. Looking inside, the young theologue was surprised to see the vestry full of little girls. They were having a prayer meeting! Furthermore, he noted, there was not a grown-up in the crowd.

He had barely time to note that not one of them was more than eight or nine when the tiny tot returned, empty-handed.

"Ah canna reach it, sir!" she said.

"But what's going on here?" asked the American, his hurry forgotten.

"It's a wheen o' us lassies prayin,'" she answered. "Will ye no' come in and get it yersel', please?"

As Hammond carefully stepped inside, a little girl who had been leading the others in prayer sensed the intrusion and finished off quickly. But another silver-tongued youngster began to pray in such simple, yet profound, petitions that tears rushed to Hammond's eyes. He quickly took his coat from the peg and hurried away.

What did it mean? How could little children pray like that? What had brought them together without adult prompting?

The answer struck Payson Hammond with the force of a tornado.

Of course! They were born again!

They were just as thoroughly converted as he had been a dozen years earlier in the Connecticut Valley!

That day in Musselburgh Payson Hammond made a vow. If God would confirm in blessing what seemed to be His clear direction, he would devote his entire life to the winning of children for Jesus Christ! As a result, Hammond was used of God to sweep thousands of children in Britain and the United States to the gates of glory. He was assisted by the winsome genius of a rugged individual named Josiah Spiers, who knew no other world than the merry, uncluttered world of children. Spiers became the founder of the Children's Special Service Mission of England.

The mantle that fell on J. Irvin Overholtzer in the twentieth century came to him from faithful predecessors. Far back in the eighteenth century, Count Ludwig von Zinzendorf, spiritual leader of the Moravians, proclaimed the Gospel to the children.

John Wesley, converted through the Moravians, clearly saw the need for child evangelism. "Unless we take care of the rising generation," he said, "the present revival of religion will be *res unius actatis* — it will only last the age of a man." Like Zinzendorf, Wesley laid great stress on work among children.

Matthew Henry, renowned British divine who authored world-famous Bible commentaries, said: "The tender regard Christ has for His Church extends itself to every particular member, not only to the whole family but to every child of the family. . . . Our Saviour warns all people, as they will answer at their own peril, not to put any stumbling block in the way of His little ones."

Robert Murray McCheyne, Scottish preacher of the early 1800's, believed too that "youth is converting time." He said: "Most that are ever saved fly to Christ when young."

F. B. Meyer, Bible teacher and writer, was convinced of the importance of child evangelism. He said, "I am increasingly enamored of the work among children. They have not to unlearn those habits of doubt and misconception which hinder so many from accepting the Gospel. It is natural for them to trust One whom they cannot see, to give Him their choicest treasures, to conform themselves to His sweet life. None but those who have worked with children could credit the readiness with which they receive the Gospel. . . . There is everything in our Saviour to charm and attract children, and His Gospel does not present difficulties to their simple faith. The Lord told us to become as little children that we might enter His kingdom. Surely, then, little children themselves have not far to go; 'only a step to Jesus.'"

Charles Haddon Spurgeon, dean among preachers, said: "You do not thoroughly know any truth till you can put it before a child so that he can see it." He told his people that in trying to make a little child understand the doctrine of the atonement "you will get clearer views of it yourselves!"

Spurgeon hoped that God would revive His church and restore her to her ancient faith by "a gracious work among the children. . . . If we would bring into our churches a large influx, how it would tend to quicken the sluggish blood of the supine and sleepy! Child Christians tend to keep the house alive. . . . Do not flatter the child with delusive rubbish about his nature being good and needing to be developed. Tell him that he must be born again."

Evangelist D. L. Moody, a firm believer in child evangelism, wrote E. Payson Hammond begging him to come and hold evangelistic meetings for children in his church in Chicago. "You do not know how much infidelity there is in the church in regard to children's conversions," he noted.

Almost prophetically, Moody added, "But thank God, there is a bright day coming."

Moody told Hammond he was praying that "you may yet live to preach in every city in this country." Whether or not this was fulfilled, we do not know. But we do know that in the turbulent twentieth century that followed, God raised up a man who touched every major city in the United States, Canada and Latin America for Christ and the children. And his life and writings ministered to the whole world in fulfillment of the Saviour's command, "Let the children come."

The Indomitable
Mr. O

The fact that my father would make such a long and hazardous trip for the sake of conscience made a great impression on my young heart.

1

Over the Hills to Tomorrow

Cannon fire was cutting a swath of destruction across Georgia in 1864, the third year of the Civil War, when a cry went up from General Sherman for more men to crush the South.

The call drifted back to the desk of President Abraham Lincoln . . . spread quickly through the valleys and hills of the North . . . and reached to the broad plains where it cropped out in bold newspaper headlines: "NORTH TO DRAFT SOLDIERS FOR SHERMAN."

In the flickering glow of a kitchen lantern, farmer Samuel Overholtzer held his newspaper closer to the light and frowned as he squinted at the text. What he saw alarmed him.

"Come here, Maria!" he called.

His little wife dried her hands on a towel and hurried to his side. Silently she followed his finger down the column of news. "What does it mean?"

"It means the government will soon be conscripting soldiers — even from among our Brethren community."

Sam got up and thoughtfully stroked his beard. "It's a sin, Maria. Brethren can't go to war and fight," the twenty-four-year-old farmer exclaimed. He sighed and folded the paper. "We've got to move."

"But Sam, we're just getting settled! And the children . . ."

"We must move West," he interrupted, "all the way West!"

They were up before dawn the next morning, carrying buckets to the barn for the milking. Powdery dew glistened in the lantern's glow as they strode across the yard. Their shoes left twin footprints on the turf. Now and then a rooster crowed in the stillness and the cows moaned and stamped at the meadow rail.

To the young couple, their farm was beautiful. The black loam of Carroll County, in northwest Illinois — much like the alluvial soil of Lancaster County, Pennsylvania, where both Samuel Ashton Overholtzer and Maria Elizabeth Harnish Overholtzer were born — was beginning to yield under their patient planting and cultivation. Three children, two boys and a girl, had been born into their family. One boy, Ezra, had died at only five weeks of age.

Maria carried the life of a fourth child. Sam had single-handedly delivered both of the children who were sleeping peacefully in the house.

Dawn began to shimmer in the east. From the stables Maria could see the outline of her house. She paused and gazed at it longingly. Would she be able to leave it? Could they make it over the dangerous trail before her baby was born?

Head-wagging neighbors would give her little comfort.

"There's a civil war on, you know," they would warn. "The government is hard put to prosecute the Indians. Massacres are nothing unusual."

"There's no doctor on the trail," others would remind them. And still others: "What if there's drought in California?"

Maria turned to watch her husband. His movements were steady, his firm jaw set. There wasn't a reckless bone in his lithe, young body. Sam had taken a bold step for God and conscience. Surely God would go with them. Surely their venture would not be in vain!

The farm sold quickly. The Overholtzers bought a covered wagon. Carefully they packed it with flour, corn, cured meats and water. Sam also took along a tin can of sweet crackers. They would play a very important part in the trek west. He arranged to join a wagon train of thirty-five families.

One morning in April, 1864, the teams were hitched, the wagons ready to go. Sam was elected to be the leader.

He gathered all together: the men, their wives and the children. Joining them in the solemn farewell were saddened relatives and friends.

Then a prayer . . . clearing of throats . . . some handkerchiefs appeared . . . goodbyes . . .

They were off.

Hardly fifty miles away, the party crossed the great "continental divide," the Mississippi River. Now it was West, ever West, into the unknown vastness.

On and on they rolled over virgin soil, for centuries untilled.

By day they watched for water and for game. By night they drew their wagons into a circle, built a fire with scraps of wood picked up along the trail and posted a guard.

Time after time they came upon gruesome scenes of Indian savagery. In several camps the red men had killed the entire party and taken their horses.

Would they make it safely across? There was many a serious moment for Sam Overholtzer as he guided the wagon train day after day, day after day, along the weary journey.

As the wagons jogged over the trail, Maria began to grow heavy with child. Scarcely over five feet tall, this plucky little black-haired woman rode beside her husband with a rifle at her side, ready to shoot game for her little family.

Sam took special precautions as he led the wagon train through treacherous Indian settlements. And with his tin of sweet crackers, a delicacy to the Indians, he was able to make acceptable peace offerings.

One day the slow-moving caravan was halted by a large mass of swampy water. Beyond the mossy bog were rich banks of green grass needed for the horses. It was Sam's plan to drive the wagons right through the water to the grassy knoll so the horses could feed. But the Indians nearby, who had become friendly through Sam's sweet gift, warned that one sip of the water could kill an animal.

To avoid the risk, Sam waded into the marsh, cut the grass and waded back with it through water up to his waist. To his dying day he was plagued with stiffness in his legs. Years later his children saw their father trying to soak out the soreness with a solution from the new leaves of the eucalyptus tree, so prevalent in Southern California.

One morning as Sam crawled out of his wagon to hitch up the horses, he found three of them writhing in pain. In a few hours they were dead. The Overholtzers were far from their destination with only one horse to finish the journey. They were stranded!

Maria began to cry.

"Alkali water," Sam said. "That last pond must have been contaminated."

Sadly he pulled off their harnesses and abandoned them to the birds of prey.

By the good hand of Providence they were able to trade the one surviving horse for two little mules, and once again the train moved west.

Month after month wore on. Would the trail never end? One cleared mountain range yielded to another. And the swamps to cross . . . the marshes . . . the rivers . . .

The men did not dare to travel the unfamiliar trail at night, and the heat of the day was stifling.

On and on creaked the big wheels of the lumbering Conestogas.

Suddenly one day, in the area now known as Reno, Nevada, Sam called a halt.

It was Maria! All the women came running to help. But it was Sam, the wagon-train leader, as he had done for his other three, who delivered this his fourth child. The date was September 8, 1864. Less than two months later, on October 31, this territory would become a state. The Overholtzers appropriately named their son Michael Nevada.

Soon the train would approach the dreaded Donner Pass in the high Sierra Nevadas where many of their traveling predecessors had perished.

Would they be able to scale those massive mountains?
How would the little mule team fare?

The travel-weary party found that their wagons could not be squeezed through the narrow trails. They had to be dismantled and lowered, piece by piece, over the precipices. They made it, just before the treacherous winter snows set in, which come early in these high altitudes.

At last, the expansive fertile Sacramento Valley lay before them, their destination! They had made it without a single loss of life in the whole party! Theirs was a "God-protected camp" Sam would later tell his children.

Bidding the other members of his party farewell and committing them to the care of God, Sam went west of Sacramento, to Yolo County, to claim one hundred sixty acres of rich land, a government homestead, along the Sacramento River. Others went farther north — to Oregon and Washington.

All were grateful for God's provision and protection over the thousands of miles they had traveled in their six-month-long journey from their home in the East.

Sam ran his fingers through the rich soil. *Ah, this will bear well! Just like the rich black loam back in Carroll County, Illinois!* He could hardly wait to harvest a crop.

But he was in for bitter disappointment. With levees not yet built, the Sacramento mercilessly overflowed with winter rains, inundating not only fields but houses where animals were sheltered. Tree houses were built to accommodate pigs and chickens, with Sam feeding his stock by boat!

The family had to be moved to higher ground until the waters had subsided.

After enduring these floods for three years, Sam moved his family farther south, to San Joaquin County, to a ranch near the town of Banta. Here such severe drought plagued him, he could raise one good crop only every three or four years.

It was man against earth in a new, stubborn wilderness. Severe privations were shared by all the family.

One of the daughters recalls a certain Christmas morning when the children came to the table to find a pair of very sober parents. There were no gifts, only a raw potato beside each child's plate as a Christmas remembrance. The children understood.

More sons and daughters were born to the Brethren pioneers. Then one summer day in 1877, on July 20, the seventh son in a family that would number thirteen children appeared. They named him Jesse Irvin. He too was destined to become a pioneer. He would be remembered — not for conquering a piece of hostile land — but for staking out a spiritual claim for the hearts of children in every corner of the world.

I must talk to someone about my deep need. Should I talk to the preacher? . . . my Sunday school teacher? . . . my father?

2

Why Not Me?

Green patches of wheat and barley, now turned yellow, stretched far off to the purple mountains that hugged the peaceful Sacramento Valley.

Here and there little clouds of dust spiraled up as harvesters swarmed across the fields cutting and sacking grain. Daniel Houser, one of the Dunkards, as the Brethren were called, had invented a monstrous combine that could cut, thresh and bag the grain — harvesting as much as one hundred acres a day! The machine was so heavy it required a dozen teams of horses to pull it across the level field.

To little Jesse it was a frightful giant that moved onto the ranch each year. He watched it with apprehension.

Near the back kitchen door one lazy summer day, Jesse

was playing in the shade of a peach tree when he heard a strange sound.

Running to the fence he pressed his face against it and watched pop-eyed as four horses on the gallop, pulling a wagonful of farm hands, came thundering toward the barn. Far in the distance black smoke billowed up from angry yellow flames. The wheat field was on fire!

His father reined the horses to a pounding halt beside the well as the men leaped off in search of barrels. Throwing them on the wagon they scooped water out of the well and the horse troughs, then clung to the wagon as it raced back again to the fields.

One barrel overturned. Sam yelled, "Let it go!"

When Jesse saw the fire sweeping across the grain fields, he rushed to the kitchen. "Ma! Ma!" he cried. "We'll all be burned! We'll all be burned!"

Maria bent down to comfort her son. But she too was worried. The whole valley was in danger of burning. Praying all the while, she kept a solemn vigil with her children. Late that night the men, their faces blackened, staggered in. They had won the battle.

The blaze had been started by a small boy playing with matches in his father's hay barn. From the barn the flames leaped to the grain fields. Farmers fought the flames by soaking grain sacks and beating the wheat ahead of the blaze. It was a scene little Jesse would never forget.

In 1882, when Jesse turned five, he received a piece of news that made his little heart dance. He and his one-year-old sister Carrie would accompany his mother on her first visit back home to Illinois! Five years after Sam Overholtzer had crossed the country with his little family, in 1869, the transcontinental railroad had joined East and West. It would carry them with lightning speed over the dusty wagon trail — this time in only a few days instead of six months!

[25]

What did a child of five remember of such a journey?

Passengers with pistols which they used to fire at prairie dogs as the train moved along . . . the mighty Mississippi River, certainly "too wide to see across" . . . relatives that swarmed around the station in Illinois to greet Maria whom they hadn't seen for eighteen years . . . an unjust crack on the knuckles from his grandfather who mistakenly thought Jesse was interfering with his sister's play . . . the farewell gathering in Illinois where guests sang the mournful tune:

> I'm going home
> No more to roam
> No more to sin and sorrow,
> No more to wear the brow of care,
> I'm going home tomorrow.

And then . . . "All aboard for California!"

The hiss of steam, the flying cinders, the landscape whizzing by, the long days on hard seats and then . . . home!

While Jesse was gone, a measles epidemic had swept through the Overholtzer household. Sam had had to nurse his sick brood and care for the house and farm while Maria and their two children were away.

Now Jesse quickly caught the measles and he had to be isolated upstairs away from the rest of the family. It was quite a jolt for the young traveler who had so recently been the object of lavish attention by his Illinois relatives. His sisters and brothers remember the loud wails that drifted down the staircase from imprisoned Jesse:

"Nobody loves me anymore!"

A year passed and Jesse found himself skipping down the dirt road with his brothers and sisters a half mile to "Old Jerusalem School." The one-room institution, built by his father and other pioneers, served from fifty to sixty youngsters who were taught by teachers usually hailing from Stockton, the county seat. One teacher taught all grades.

Students could advance as rapidly as they wished through the courses in reading, writing, arithmetic, geography and history.

Some students walked three miles to school. Many rode horses. One boy who regularly came to school on the back of a burro furnished hours of fun by letting the youngsters ride his "wheels." But if the burro decided too many had climbed on his back, he would sit down and let them slide in a heap at his heels.

The Overholtzer children were pink-cheeked and hearty from rugged work and play. They often picked gooseberries on hills above the farm and scouted the banks of the San Joaquin River five miles away for wild blackberries.

Young Jesse loved the ranch. Working with its soil was like working with the stuff of Paradise. In later years he would grow large beds of flowers to fill the house with their fragrance.

As a lad of six Jesse begged his father for a plot of ground he could call his own.

At last Sam assigned to him a tiny plot and gave him radish seed. This he knew would germinate and sprout quickly.

Jesse carefully smoothed the ground and dropped in the tiny seeds.

The following morning he hurried out, expecting to see radishes! Keenly disappointed, he dug down to find the seed exactly as he had planted it. He dug up the radishes three or four times in his impatience, then forgot about them.

One day he visited his "farm." There to his surprise were radish stalks! They were yellow and sickly from their stormy beginning, but they grew; and eventually they shared the secrets of growth and the rewards of patience with an eager little boy.

Jesse also loved the tiny "library" of their ranch home. At the age of four he began opening books and studying the pictures. The big family Bible, profusely illustrated, yielded the most drama to his youthful eyes.

"Many were the evenings that I lay on the floor with this Bible, poring over the pictures," he later recalled. "No one told me Bible stories in those days. The pictures were in chronological order with a brief description under each one. I learned quite a connected history of the Bible that way."

Later, when he was able to read for himself, he frequently perused an edition of *Fox's Book of Martyrs*.

"I read it again and again," he recalled. "It told vividly of the martyrdom of the heroes of faith during the Reformation period. I knew nothing of Catholicism and Protestantism; but men and women being tortured for their faith in Christ never failed to inspire me. Seeing them reject every offer of deliverance if they would renounce their faith left impressions that were never erased."

A little "preventive" evangelism then would have spared the young man years of heartache later on as he struggled to find forgiveness of sin and assurance of salvation.

In 1704, many years earlier, another boy of only four, who later became Count Zinzendorf of the Moravians, wrote a letter to Jesus. He tossed it out of the castle window where he lived, for the wind to carry away. It read: "Dear Saviour, do Thou be mine, and I will be thine."

As an adult this dashing figure who gave up wealth and status to serve the Lord Jesus stated as his life's motto: "I have one passion: it is Jesus, Jesus only!"

It is hardly too much to affirm that Count Zinzendorf did more than any other man to redeem the eighteenth century from the reproach of barrenness in relation to evangelical teaching and work. At this very early age of four, he had been given full assurance of salvation.

But young Jesse Overholtzer stumbled on in his childish manner, searching for answers to the many questions which were forming in his mind. One after another he brought these to his mother. Finally she lost patience with him.

Many of them she was unable to answer to his satisfaction. He asked questions of anyone who would listen, but the answer usually came back: "You aren't old enough to understand."

That means, Jesse thought, *they don't know the answers themselves!*

The year 1885 was Jesse's last at Old Jerusalem School, for news of the citrus boom in Southern California had reached the ears of his father.

That year Sam Overholtzer rode the Southern Pacific Railroad to Los Angeles, and then traveled twenty miles east by wagon to Covina where he purchased eighty acres of rich, sandy loam on the J. S. Phillips tract.

There was no bank in Covina and no one living knows how this Brethren farmer, unassisted, financed his new claim, built a large, two-story dwelling (with a bathtub!) and set out groves of orange trees on the broad slopes of his new land. Sam spoke little and worked hard. Once, for the sake of conscience and the love of God, he had risked his life to establish a home in a free land; now he was willing to lay his future on the line for a new beginning in a burgeoning boom town.

No one was happier to leave for Covina than Jesse. The eight-year-old boy who had lived so long under conviction of sin thought that perhaps a new life in a new community would miraculously dispel the doubts and fears that had plagued his soul.

In Covina his father established membership in a congregation which became the mother church in that area for the Dunkards, later known as the Church of the Brethren.

"Each of us had a Bible or Testament," Jesse recalled, "and we children rarely missed Sunday school and church services.

"The teaching and preaching from the Bible . . . the atmosphere of the church and godly neighbors, and especially the Christian lives of my father and mother greatly influenced me. Joining the church and being baptized were constantly emphasized.

"I often did wrong and I was usually sorry afterwards," he said. "I had not been taught to pray and do not recall ever praying. Praying and religion were for grown-ups, not for children. Children were to 'be good.' When they were old enough they could 'join the church.'

"How I longed to be 'right with God,' to be ready to die!" he once wrote as he recalled the agony of his soul. "The way of salvation was never made plain to me, for I was considered too young. No boy of twelve had ever joined the church, as far as I knew.

"Every day conviction of sin became greater. I believe this was the Holy Spirit although at the time I knew nothing of the Holy Spirit. I lost interest in play. I would lie awake at night thinking of how bad I was. I even lost my appetite! What should I do? What could I do?"

Finally, in desperation, he decided to talk with someone. "The preacher? He had never baptized a boy of twelve. I was sure he could not help me. The Sunday school teacher? He had never taught that boys of twelve could come to Jesus. I was sure he would turn me away."

His father was a devout man. He had often spoken warmly about the church and the preacher, but he never talked about Jesus or salvation — or even about prayer.

"I could not talk to my father," he said, "so I decided to go to my mother. I loved her dearly, and I knew she loved me. I felt she was one of the best Christians I knew, but I was afraid to discuss a subject that seemed to be taboo — the question of personal salvation."

Twelve-year-old Jesse gathered his courage. He thought somehow that joining the church was synonymous with "getting right with God." With fear in his heart and trembling lips he watched his chance and blurted out, "I want to join the church."

Maria Overholtzer stopped working and came over to the corner of the kitchen where he was standing. Looking at him tenderly she said, "Son, you are too young."

"She did not ask why I had wanted to join the church," Mr. Overholtzer said many years later. "She was in bondage to the teaching of those times. Even my mother said I was too young. I had to wait.

"I learned the fear of God but not His love. I saw the terribleness of sin and God's judgment upon it, but I learned nothing of the Gospel of grace — and no one taught me that Gospel."

A cloud of discouragement settled on the lad. "If I'm lost and can't get saved, then I can't get any more lost," he reasoned.

Conviction was passing. Anyone who had known how could have led him to Christ. The pleasant little chap turned prankster and later brought much grief to his parents.

"I'll just sin if I want to," he told himself.

If I was too young to be saved, why not get all the pleasure out of sin I thought others were enjoying? I closed the door on my narrow world and stepped out on the broad road.

3

Slamming the Castle Gate

Covina felt good to the eleven Overholtzers who had scorched and sizzled in the dry mid-state ranchlands of California. Golden fruit began appearing on the green groves stretching in long rows beneath the white peak of Mt. Baldy. Wild flowers like the poppy, lupine and brodea bloomed profusely in this storybook land. News of the attractive valley drifted back to the East where many were quick to respond to its call. In those days, families could ride to California on railroad boxcars for one dollar, but if they decided not to stay they would have to pay full passenger fare back home.

Among the migrators were scores of Brethren families who traveled in colonies. Dr. Gladys E. Muir, of La Verne

College, writing the seventy-five-year history of the Brethren school that Sam Overholtzer helped establish, said:

> Brethren had a tendency to move in groups and settle in colonies, probably because they were German-speaking in the beginning and there were some language and custom barriers separating them from the rest of the community. Then, too, they had come to believe that colonization was the best method of evangelism — the lonely preacher, unsupported by his brethren, did not have as good an opportunity to 'enlarge the Kingdom' as the member of a community who lived in warm and satisfying fellowship. This explains why the railroads were quite successful when they employed agents to encourage Brethren emigration to the West. They were likely to secure a whole colony of them instead of a few individuals.

Jesse felt himself a prisoner of the Brethren colony in Covina. While the work in the orange groves was open and free, the spiritual life of the church was not. The German Brethren tolerated no infractions of the church's rules and were "overstrict about worldliness."

Jesse recalled: "It was wrong to go to a children's party or to an entertainment. Children's parties were held occasionally in the best homes of members of other churches, but I was not allowed to go to these. Soon this was known and I was no longer invited. I was not willing to follow the standards of the church since I was not allowed to join it. Resentful, I sought pleasures and companionship elsewhere."

Who drafted the strict rules of the church? They came partly from the arbitrary whims of its ruling elders, partly from the long battle against worldliness which characterized the Anabaptists of Europe in their complete break with the state church.

The *Large Chronicle of the Hutterian Brethren* preserves the record of these pietists from whom the German Dunkards were descended. In protest of the practice of infant baptism, the "errors" of current reformers, and to symbolize their complete break with the state, these Germans dared to form a church after what they conceived to be the New Testament pattern.

According to W. R. Estep in *The Anabaptist Story*, the Brethren emphasized "the absolute necessity of a personal commitment to Christ as essential to salvation and a prerequisite to baptism."

But in the rigid Brethren society of the pioneers, joining the church, baptism and obeying the rules of the church in the smallest detail received the greatest stress.

Jesse missed the teaching of a "personal commitment to Christ" in the strict Brethren society. He had sought a vital relationship with his Saviour but was guided instead by laws without spirit. He was to stress to his co-workers later, "The letter killeth, but the spirit giveth life."

"I rebelled against the social straitjacket," he said. "Since I was not allowed to attend the innocent social gatherings, I began running with boys who frequented the local poolroom. I soon knew cards and dice in addition to pool. Foul language and some drinking were common at the poolroom."

The years between 1889 and 1897, from ages twelve to twenty, were "full of dark memories — would that they could be forgotten."

Jesse carried his rebellion into the classroom at Center School, Covina. He was a born leader and he drew other boys with him into mischievous plots against the establishment.

In Union School he joined a "military" company which had regular drills during the lunch hour. Jesse wasn't a member long before he began striving to be captain. He stirred up opposition against the leader, staged a "court martial" and took over the post.

Adjoining the school grounds in Covina was a large patch

of trees bearing chickasaw plums that students were allowed to pick. Many a pitched battle was waged by the military company with wild plums for ammunition.

When Captain Overholtzer took command, he had plans for conquest. One day their male teacher was called out to see a battle between the "military" and the "civilian" members of the school. Then suddenly, by pre-arrangement, the "soldiers" turned on the teacher and began pelting him with green plums. As he ran for the schoolhouse they followed him, bombing and strafing all the way. Captain Overholtzer was punished severely. "The sound whipping was deserved," he concluded later.

Jesse's repeated pranks brought down on him the wrath of a neighboring farmer, so the youngster decided to get even. One moonlight night he and some "partners in crime" laid planks to the roof of the neighbor's barn and coaxed his cow on top of it. In the middle of the night the farmer heard his cow bellowing. To his amazement, he discovered the poor animal on the barn roof! Certain that Jesse Overholtzer was the mastermind behind the deed, the farmer reported it to Jesse's father. The seventh Overholtzer son was beaten severely with a horse whip.

Everything his father and mother provided was his to enjoy. But Jesse yearned for other parts and the thrills of being on his own. He could "tolerate" his family only until he was eighteen.

His younger sister, Carrie, found her mother crying one day in the kitchen.

"Ma, what's the matter?" she asked.

"Haven't you noticed? *Jesse is gone!*"

Not another word was said about the prodigal, but he felt the love of his family regardless of his misdeeds and arrogant acts.

"Only after I left did I begin to realize the depth of my mother's spirituality and her prayer life," he said. "I had disgraced the family but she loved me just the same."

The one who had left home now became the object of her special love. "She wrote me regularly in her matter-of-fact way, whether I answered or not. Between the lines were urgent appeals for me to return home.

"Her letters were full of the things of Christ — just the things that were lacking when I was seeking salvation. My mother had fallen ill and was the victim of more and greater suffering, but her spiritual life had deepened and her prayer life had become wonderful." This change in her life had largely come about through her reading of the classic devotional work of Hannah Whitall Smith, *The Christian's Secret of a Happy Life*.

The hard work on his father's farm was light compared with the toil he now endured. "I had no special training," he said, "so all I could get was heavy physical labor. I was no longer the son of a leading citizen who was a director in the local bank, of the water company and of the Orange Growers Association. . . ."

Jesse's first job was the shuttling of heavy sacks of coal in a rowboat at a river depot. But when he dropped a bag of coal into thirty feet of water, he was fired and had to look for another job. It came from a railroad line which offered him a position as section hand, swinging a pick and shovel all day. The prodigal was being brought to himself through the grimy sweat of unrelenting labor.

He thought of those three hearty meals a day back on the farm and the good bed that had cost him nothing. "Now I could hardly earn enough to pay for my board and room. There was little money left over to pay for the sinful pleasures which I had dreamed I would enjoy away from parental restraint."

One day at a beach party along the Pacific Ocean he decided to plunge in for a refreshing swim. The first wave made him shiver. The next one was invigorating and soon he was past the breakers into the calm swirl of the ocean.

Suddenly a strong undertow caught his body and began pulling the helpless swimmer out to sea.

"I was choked into panic," he recalled, "certain at one moment that all was over and that I would drown. Then, instantly the undertow ceased and I swam safely to shore. I felt at that moment God had delivered me through my mother's prayers."

While the seventh son was absent from home Derius, an older brother, had made the decision to receive Christ as his Saviour. He persuaded his father to let him begin a family altar. This drew the Overholtzers closer together in prayer for wayward Jesse.

A spiritual warmth settled on the family circle. The dozen or so hired men working on the Overholtzer ranch all had to attend family prayer before breakfast. Prior to these days the Bible had been rarely opened. Now it was given prominence in all family activities. Father Overholtzer began reading the Bible openly, sitting in his highly prized old armchair. Both Bible and chair had crossed the plains with him. Both he kept until he died.

Although these were prosperous days for the Overholtzers, Sam and Maria were miserable without Jesse, whose stubborn pride kept him from coming home.

His mother suffered greatly from colitis. The troublesome inflammation was making her an invalid. She wanted desperately to see her Jesse Irvin.

"Please go to him and ask him to come home," she begged her husband. "Once more, ask him."

Sam needed no prodding.

The next morning he harnessed his best horse to a buggy, put on his suit, set his hat and was off to talk to his boy. He found Jesse in a cheap boarding house.

The boy was shocked to see his stern father at the door of his room. The greeting was matter-of-fact.

"Come in, Pa."

Mr. Overholtzer came quickly to the point of his call.

"If you will come home, Jesse, I'll send you to college. That's all your mother and I ask — just come back and live with us."

It was a good offer, but still Jesse refused to return home. He was living on "husks," but he was determined to seek his fortune alone. He sent his father away sad and disappointed.

As the evangelist preached, one after another of my grounds for rejecting Christ was swept away.

4

Liberation!

Jesse watched his father climb into the familiar old family buggy. A pang of regret stole over him. There was still time to call out. One word from him would have brought a smile to that old face and smoothed the worried wrinkles on the brow . . .

Jesse took a deep breath. He ran his fingers through his hair and cast a glance at the sky. *I've got lots of living to do yet,* he said to himself. He went inside and closed the door.

One hard job followed another. Employers were glad to get the young farmer with the strong back, but Jesse had to take whatever they would pay. He wanted to save some money and enter the profession of law, which attracted his interest. But it seemed the harder he worked the more it took to live. He was becoming desperate. In his daydreams he pictured himself with his parents, surrounded by plenty. Still he refused to return home humiliated. He *must* make some achievements; he *must* go home with his head high, looking like the successful young man his heart yearned to be.

The "Gay 90's" had arrived, but they were gloomy, crushing days for many in the San Gabriel Valley. The nation was caught in the grip of an economic depression. Many new residents of Covina lost their entire holdings. Throughout the decade people were pulling up stakes and heading back East — all this while Covina's oranges, prunes and plums were winning first prize at the Chicago World's Fair.

With the hordes of unemployed came the hobos and tramps. There still were but few banks and money was scarce. Bartering was common, and there was cordiality and cooperation among the settlers. The newspaper *Argus*, published in Covina, relates that when Ed Worrall was too ill to set out 11,000 strawberry plants, forty neighbors showed up to do the job for him.

With failing investments and a shortage of cash, crime increased. People carried their money on their person, hid it in the house or buried it in a nearby field.

One of the most notorious and baffling thieves was a phantom called "Old Stocking Foot" who pilfered many an unsuspecting house at night but never was caught.

When older men with families became desperate for work, young men like Jesse Overholtzer found it harder and harder to find employment. His need for food and room continued, however, and life's hard realities began closing in.

"What a fool I am!" Jesse murmured one evening as he munched his meager victuals. "I am the son of a prosperous family who love me and want me to come home, but my pride won't let me! What a fool! What a fool!"

The next step was to pack and return home, unless . . .

That's it! He had a married sister in Pasadena who would take him in! If he walked the twenty miles west, he would get to Anna Louise and her husband.

"*Pasadena, here I come!*"

Jesse presented himself at the door of Mr. and Mrs. John Billheimer without a cent, without a job and with diminishing self-respect.

"*Jesse!*" his sister "Lutie" exclaimed as she drew him into the house. "You look starved!"

Jesse was fed and given a room. The following day his brother-in-law, in the lumber business, gave him a job at the mill. Handling planks thirty-two feet by sixteen inches was a school of hard learning.

When money began coming in once more, ambitions returned. Jesse decided to start climbing for his most coveted goal: to become a lawyer.

His brother-in-law used his influence to get him into the law office of one of Pasadena's best attorneys. But the association was short-lived.

Reading Blackstone seemed pretty dull to one who had left home to get thrills, he admitted.

Then came the lawyer's fatherly advice: "You don't have enough education. You must go to college."

Now it meant leaving the City of Roses and returning home to admit to his father that he was wrong . . . that he must accept his offer of education . . . that he had sown the wind and reaped the whirlwind.

Yet it was a happy young man who stepped off the Santa Fe iron horse in Covina to rejoin his family. The prodigal found a warm welcome in his father's house. The days of husks and failure were over. Ahead, only a few weeks away, was the opening of a whole new life in college.

Although Jesse's father had no scholastic training, he was intensely interested in education. He was one of four men who founded Lordsburg College, first Brethren institution of learning in the West.

A fancy hotel in Lordsburg, which later became La Verne College and thrives today in the town of that name near Covina, was built in the boom by an Easterner named Lord. He opened the premises just as economic disaster was sending settlers out of the area instead of bringing them in. The hotel was secured as a building in which to open the college.

The freshman selected as courses business and the Bible, plus "elocution."

He was prominent on campus. After all, he was the son of a founder. But he let it be known from the start that he had little truck with the church.

Jesse, of the class of 1899, was invited by classmates to a series of evangelistic meetings in the college chapel. Again and again the dapper young man refused, boasting to his buddies:

"I can get along without that stuff. Come on! We didn't come to school for religion!"

The spiritual emphasis week wore on. One by one, students were getting right with God.

Finally "out of respect to the college" Jesse picked a night and went to the meetings.

As the evangelist preached, the auditorium seemed to become hot. Jesse wished he could leave and return to his room. He wanted to hang on to the old life, not to "succumb to religious pressure."

His deeds began to pass before him. *Is that what I want?* he thought, *that old life with its frustration and worry?*

The evangelist pressed on. One after another of Jesse's grounds for rejecting Christ was swept away. Finally, when the invitation was given, he was the first to respond.

"I was *such* a sinner that I came 'all of grace' and threw myself on the mercy of God," he said later. "I not only accepted Jesus as my personal Saviour but surrendered my life to Him as best I knew."

The spiritual housecleaning of young Jesse caused an excited stir on campus and in the church. Once he had majored in pleasurable pursuits. Now he buckled down to his studies. Once he had wanted to be a lawyer. Now he made plans to be a missionary. He threw all his energies into his new commitment. "When Jesse did anything," his sister Celia recalled, "he did it with his whole heart!"

After Jesse was converted, he wouldn't submit to baptism until he had straightened out an old grievance with one of his father's hired hands, walking eight miles to do so.

"I had hated this man — hated the very ground he walked on," Jesse said. "The man was dumbfounded when I confronted him and asked his forgiveness. I told him I had accepted Christ as my Saviour and asked him to forgive me for all the wrong things I had said about him."

Working alone at a fruit stand, in his desperate plight he had taken money from the till a number of times to keep from starving. Now he wrote to his former employer and confessed the theft. He returned four times the amount he had taken. The employer sent back a portion of it in his letter of forgiveness.

Jesse was baptized and joined the Church of the Brethren.

"I received a blessed witness of the Holy Spirit," he testified. "My zeal in Bible study and witnessing consumed me. I offered myself for full-time Christian work, feeling I had a call from the Lord."

As Jesse enrolled for his junior year at Lordsburg College, his mother began failing fast. She had prayed long and lived to see the conversion of her wandering boy.

On February 7, 1897, Maria Harnish Overholtzer, the sturdy pioneer who had gladly left a comfortable home for the dangerous trail west, was called Home.

Before she died, Maria summoned all her eleven remaining children into her room. As she looked lovingly from one to the other of them she pleaded softly, "Meet me in Heaven . . . meet me in Heaven."

The Brethren people did not demonstrate their deep-seated religious belief in those days, but his mother's departing word remained in Jesse's heart.

"My mother bore the sweetest testimony for Christ that night," he said. "Just before she lost consciousness, her face lit up with glory light which was beyond question a supernatural light. This vision of mother's face, reflecting a bit of Heaven, has been used of God again and again to keep me true to the Lord's will, even when the going became very, very hard."

There to comfort him on the day of his mother's death was a second lady who was to influence the life of young Overholtzer. She was a spunky little girl from South Haven, Michigan. Anna Ewing had come West with her parents. Jesse had met her in Covina.

Jesse and Anna were married on August 10, 1897, in Covina, a year before they were graduated from Lordsburg College. Young Overholtzer bravely titled his valedictory address "Success!"

Anna became the mother of Overholtzer's nine children — six girls and three boys.

"And a wonderful mother she was!" he often recalled.

The harder I tried to observe the rules of my denomination, the less I knew of the sweetness of the certainty of sins forgiven.

5

Beards, Bonnets and an Empty Soul

The first days of marriage for Jesse and Anna were no honeymoon. They moved into the home of Jesse's brother William to care for the five children while he and his wife went East!

Later Jesse and Anna set up housekeeping in La Verne. Nearby was Colton, where the young man began his ministry as a lay preacher, serving what was called a "mission point."

The denomination in which Overholtzer served was organized in Germany in 1708. The history of the church, the Church of the Brethren, falls into three major epochs: (1) from its organization in Germany to the new settlement in the colonies in 1777, when General Howe took Philadelphia and destroyed their printing presses; (2) from the Revolutionary War to 1850, when a great migration westward took place; and (3) from 1850 and on, during which time the small denomination became established.

Strict rules for water baptism were laid down by the Brethren in those early days. Members had to be baptized not only by immersion but by *trine* immersion — three times forward, face down.

Salvation of the soul depended on the proper baptism of the body, they believed.

Besides strict adherence to these church ordinances, members must, to the letter, obey additional rules set up at the annual meetings of the denomination. Disobedience meant loss of membership.

Ladies must wear the prescribed bonnets, not hats. Many young women lost their church membership when they appeared wearing hats!

Men must wear beards, and from Leviticus 19:27 they set up the regulation: "neither shalt thou mar the corners of thy beard." No trimming!

At one time to have carpets on the floor, unless repented of, brought expulsion from the church.

Many similar rules were heatedly debated and passed or rejected at the annual meetings. Into all of this young Preacher Overholtzer entered with great zeal, vigorously pressing each rule.

Almost without exception the ministers in that conference preached and practiced "salvation by works."

"Those who were the most strict," observed Overholtzer, "were the least spiritual. My own preaching, even in evangelistic meetings, bore little fruit. *My* converts seldom gave evidence of being born again.

"I had known the sweetness of the certainty of sins forgiven. The Holy Spirit witnessing with my spirit that I was a child of God had once been a blessed reality. Now this peace and assurance had taken wings and flown away. I did not know why, for I was *trying so hard* to obey God and to serve Him faithfully, according to the rules of my denomination."

Of the doctrine of works, Overholtzer said: "I accepted it fully — right down to the beards and the bonnets. I believed that the Bible was the very Word of God, that Jesus was God the Son, that Christ died on the cross for my sin and rose again from the grave. But I had added something to the *finished* work of Christ on the cross. Salvation was not a free gift — salvation was not by grace. I still taught, or thought I taught, justification by faith; but the way I defined faith, it included many acts of obedience to be saved. Among these works, of course, was always water baptism by the proper mode.

"If it took all this to get salvation and to keep it, then no one was saved unless he had my brand of good works.

"I soon began doubting my salvation, for I saw that if salvation was by works, only *perfect* works could be accepted by God. How well I knew that my most zealous works were not of that kind!"

After Maria's death, Sam Overholtzer began putting less stress on church rules. Now sixty-one, he was ailing from cancer of the stomach. He would not allow anyone to wait on him or care for him in any way. The only way his children could tell he was ill was by observing him at the table.

At one time the church had forbidden the taking of photographs. For most of his life Sam had followed this rule. But on a trip back to Illinois he was suddenly taken up short. *If I were killed on this trip*, he thought, *my children wouldn't have a picture of me!* He had photos taken and sent one to each of his family.

Only a few years remained for the hardy pioneer. The cancer was growing, and he found it more and more difficult to eat.

"When saved people face death," remarked his son Jesse

some years later, "everything but Christ and Him crucified falls away. It was so with my father. He was a man of few words, but as he lay dying [the year was 1900], he left this testimony none of us will ever forget: 'I am at peace with God and man.'"

But the peace with God his seventh son had experienced when he had first come to the Lord was missing.

Brother Jesse struggled on, rich in rules, but empty in soul.

God was beginning to deal with me in chastisement to bring me to the place of blessing. Everything I touched failed.

6

Prisoner of Law

Jesse's share of his father's substantial legacy tempted him to "go for broke" on several fruitless schemes. He founded a weekly newspaper called *The Sunbeam*. He invested in an unproductive mining claim. And he rode a variety of hobbies.

For a time he worked as the local agent in Colton for the Hartford Fire Insurance Company. He was also part owner in a water-purifying station.

All ventures failed, and the legacy disappeared. His disappointments drew him deeper into the church.

On Sundays, the young man wore the familiar garb of a preacher in his denomination. Often he preached three times on the Lord's day, serving without pay, as did most of the ministers in the Church of the Brethren at that time.

Brother Jesse grew a beard out of conviction. He preached softly, with a smile, but remained strict regarding the rules of his church group.

In the denomination ministers as well as officers were elected by the local congregation. Preachers were appointed first to a position called "the first degree." This authorized them to take part in limited duties, such as preaching and teaching, and to serve during Communion. The "second degree" preacher could perform marriages. The highest position gave him the privilege of attending state district meetings, with the consent of the local church.

Overholtzer steadily ascended the denominational ladder. But the stricter he became with himself and others, the less he enjoyed what he later called "the blessed witness of the Holy Spirit."

Downtown in Colton one morning Jesse happened upon an auction outside the Railway Express office. A box of unclaimed books was on the block. Books had charmed him since he was a toddler "reading" the illustrations of the old family Bible as he stretched himself out on the floor. Since then he had tasted, chewed and digested a good many of them and now saw a chance to add considerably to his library.

"Twenty-five cents!" Overholtzer shouted.

"Sold!"

He quickly paid the auctioneer and examined his purchase. There were novels and heavy documentaries and then he pulled out, of all things, *The Life of Moody.*

"That deluded evangelist!" Brother Jesse muttered. He stroked his beard as he read a page or two at random about the Chicago shoe salesman whose message had swept thousands of Americans and Britons into the Kingdom of God.

He tossed the book back into the box. *I'll not waste time reading that,* he thought to himself, little realizing the important part the book would play in his life.

The young Pennsylvania Dutchman preached harder and harder, cracking the denominational whip on every rule. To the fundamental doctrines of Scripture, he added acts of obedience as requirements for justification. His gospel of works became so complicated, he began to doubt whether he himself could "keep saved."

Few responded to his message and these gave but little evidence of being born again. They had come to Christ on the ground of works. They were told that they must do other things in addition to simply believing if they would be saved.

"They believed the preacher and failed to find Christ," he later related.

"Bonnets instead of hats . . . wood floors instead of carpeting . . . dark instead of gay clothing . . . hooks and eyes instead of buttons — I began to tire of it all, and I'm sure my people did too."

If these were the rudiments of salvation, they must change from culture to culture and from generation to generation, the preacher reasoned. Were these really what the Lord asked of His people?

If deliverance came by works, then only *perfect* works would be accepted by God, he decided. Brother Jesse longed to have his life controlled by the Spirit, no longer to be a slave to his human nature.

He felt himself a prisoner of law, reaching out for deliverance, which he thought came through more law . . . more rules . . . more decrees.

"I worked on and on, harder and harder; now so strict that in my zeal I found myself differing with almost everyone on questions of conduct and of doctrine. By this time I had a family of children and was so strict with them that they well-nigh lost their love for me — all to get salvation, to keep it, or to regain it.

"But still no blessing. There was no blessing in any department of my life. No blessing in my business and no blessing in my prayer life.

"My prayers seemed to get no higher than the ceiling. There were no answers.

"Oh, the agony of soul. I would have given my right arm to know that I was saved, to get my blessing back. I had become a bigoted Pharisee. I was trying to provide a righteousness of my own instead of believing that God had already provided this righteousness.

"I knew my Bible and could quote a great deal of it. But the texts that stressed works were my favorites. I did not know what to do with the ones that mentioned grace. They had no place in my thinking — in my theology.

"Had I been asked to define the word *grace,* I could not have done it."

As color returned to the earth in the spring of 1905, under the electric blue skies of sunny California, Jesse and Anna made a daring move. Along with eight or ten other Brethren families they went to Glenn County, in the Sacramento Valley.

For Jesse it was going home, back to the northern section of the great valley where his father had settled a generation before him.

With Anna and their three small children — Ruth, Paul and Esther — they settled on the Packer Tract, five miles west of the Sacramento River, near the little town of Willows.

Overholtzer circled his new home with trees, until it soon was completely hidden from passersby on the dirt road out front. As his family grew he added new rooms, making one of them a study where he could prepare sermons.

He had gone heavily into debt to make the move. Failing was out of the question.

The preacher-farmer became pastor of the local assembly which met in homes until a meeting house could be built.

A small clapboard sanctuary seating about fifty people was erected on a corner of a grain field belonging to Jesse's sister. Sunday school and the worship service were held in one room. The building was ringed with hitching posts for horses.

It was a strange sight to a young Portuguese man, hired to work on the Overholtzer ranch. One Sunday, curious, he decided to "join the circle of Protestants." Before migrating to America he had been told that Protestants worship the devil. He fully expected the unusual that Sunday morning. Instead Ferdinand Custer sat enthralled listening to a kind preacher, who talked fervently of the things of God.

The Portuguese immigrant was drawn to the Overholtzer family. "The Overholtzers were a closely knit family," says Custer. "They were one for all and all for one. I think they regarded me as a curiosity, but they took me in."

Custer remembers hauling a load of fruit and vegetables to town to sell on the street. He returned too late Saturday night to give his boss the money, so he handed it to him on Sunday.

"I'm sorry, Ferdy," the strict preacher said. "I can't accept money on the Lord's day. That will have to wait."

Mrs. Overholtzer, Ferdinand Custer recalls, was unusually hospitable, and she displayed an amazing amount of energy. When the fruit was ripe, she would rise with her husband at five in the morning to pick berries in the cool dawn before the stifling summer heat rose with the sun.

Jesse Overholtzer was a strict disciplinarian. He did not spare the rod, but he was not harsh. As his father had done before him, he demanded utter obedience.

"My mother was gentle," Ruth says. "She never raised her voice to her children or to anyone. 'If you can't behave,' she would say, 'I'll have to tell your father.'"

The earth responded well to the clever farmer's diligent nursing. Walnut groves and peach orchards were set out and farm crops planted and harvested between the young trees as they grew to maturity.

Melons, beans, sweet corn, mammoth blackberries and other truck crops were harvested between the long rows of fruit trees and then sold in the community or shipped to the city. Like his German ancestors in the country of his forefathers, Overholtzer farmed every inch of his twenty acres and made them blossom like a rose. He had arrived in Glenn County with his family and fifty dollars. Within five years he had developed an irrigation system on his tract, built a home, planted orchards, groves, and was receiving an annual income from his farming operation of two thousand dollars. At this time ranch foremen were being paid only fifty dollars a month. Later he developed a small canning business on his farm.

Hard work had brought prosperity in business but it did not alleviate the hunger in his soul. He continued to preach regularly each Sunday but his heart grew even more hungry.

"My pursuit of a righteousness on the basis of my own conduct was fast leading me to despair. If after sixteen years of earnest effort I was not saved, was there any reasonable prospect that I would be?

"Then what message did I have for others who wanted salvation? The best I had to offer them was an opportunity to yield to Christ in obedience and start working for their salvation as I was doing.

"I believed of course that God forgave my sins from time to time, but was I ever free from sin when I was not perfect? And what if I should die in such a state?

"I feared death. I longed to have the witness of the Holy Spirit again. I was not in the position of those who fall into the error of salvation by works before they *get* to Christ for salvation, for they have never tasted of the bliss of the Holy Spirit's witness and do not know what it is and what they are missing. But I had once enjoyed this blessing. It was agony to live without it.

"My thoughts turned to *The Life of Moody* and I was tempted to read it, though I knew I should burn it! The longer I kept it, the more I was convinced that I should read it. At last I yielded.

"I soon saw that this man had what I needed and longed for."

But Overholtzer turned his back on the message. According to his salvation-by-works standard, Moody was not saved!

"Still I could not get away from the message of that book," he related.

But God has His way of dealing with His children. Scarlet fever struck with sudden decisiveness. The whole Overholtzer ranch was quarantined. And the quarantine lasted for thirteen weeks.

Overholtzer now had plenty of time for meditation. He decided to make a complete restudy of the Bible.

"I asked the Lord for guidance as I began to study and promised Him that I would follow the truth as I found it, regardless of the cost."

The devils believe but are not saved. How may I know that I have the faith that saves?

7

Assurance on a Stepladder

The coming of spring in that year of 1914 did not lighten either the physical or spiritual load of the busy farmer.

The "Scarlet Fever" quarantine sign still hung on the front door. Busy scampering children were still under foot.

And there was a whole orchard of peach trees to be pruned. Cumbersome wood must be cut so all the energies of the tree could go to producing rich fruit.

Overholtzer trimmed trees by day and pored over the Scriptures at night.

Hour after hour he carefully assayed the Word, seeking for an answer to his spiritual dilemma. Little by little he came to the place where he was willing to be taught. It became clear to him that if his restudy of the Word was to be of any value, he must come to his investigation with an open mind.

Too, if he found that the Bible taught salvation by grace with *no* good works as a condition of salvation, it would cost him a break with his denomination. This would involve not only his ministry but nearly all his friends and relatives, for they were all members of this group and they would condemn his action.

First the Bible student listed the verses that taught salvation was by grace, a free gift.[1] Next he listed the ones that taught salvation was *not* of works.[2] Then he listed those that made it clear that salvation was by simple faith in Christ crucified, as the sinner's substitute.[3] Over against these Scriptures he set verses he had used through the years to teach salvation by works.

Then the struggle began.

While Overholtzer trimmed his peach trees, God was also at work, cutting from his life spiritual deadwood.

Up and down the ladder he went — from tree to tree; tree to tree. All the while his thoughts were: *What is the truth? Is one saved by faith alone in Jesus Christ? This is just too easy. It cannot be! It just cannot be!*

Methodical and persistent, Overholtzer memorized Scriptures he had discovered that taught salvation is by grace alone. Gradually the Word began to do its own profitable pruning. Scriptures he was sure that taught salvation is by works began to recede from the mental front lines. More and more, verses teaching salvation by grace pushed to the fore. "I literally discovered the word *grace* in the Bible,"

---

[1] Isaiah 55:1; John 4:10-14; 10:28, 29; 17:2; Romans 5:18; 6:23; Ephesians 2:8,9; Revelation 21:6; 22:17.
[2] Romans 3:20, 28; 4:4-6, 9, 10; Galatians 2:16; Ephesians 2:9; II Timothy 1:9.
[3] John 1:12; 3:14-16, 18, 36; 5:24; 6:29, 47; Acts 10:43; 13:38, 39; 15:7-9; Romans 4:16; 5:1; Galatians 3:22; Ephesians 2:8, 9; I John 5:13.

he said, a word which previously was not in his frame of reference.

"At first it seemed that these verses could not possibly mean that a sinner could be instantaneously saved by a simple act of faith without any added or preceding good works or reformation of conduct."

But the more he studied them, the more the Holy Spirit convicted him that this was the truth.

"Now I stood at the parting of the ways. I was at last convinced with my head that salvation was secured alone by believing."

But another great problem arose.

"If I should accept this truth, how could I face my people and tell them I had been teaching them error all the years? I was afraid my church would repudiate me and I would be cast adrift with a large family and little means and no friends."

It was a terrible struggle, lasting for days. The battle went on apace.

"It seemed too good to be true that God would save me without waiting for me to quit my sins or before I had rendered any service."

One day, high on the ladder snapping off the dry branches, he saw it. Like a mountain avalanche that gains speed and power the further it descends, the truths of God broke loose and completely toppled his opposition.

"*It must be so! It must be so!*" he suddenly cried out.

Then, "*It is so. I accept it for myself.*"

His heart and mind were calmed as to his bosom he embraced the truth: "For by grace are ye saved through faith; and that not of yourselves: it is the gift of God." His soul was flooded with the Holy Spirit's witness.

"I was too happy for words. The joy bells were ringing in my heart. I knew I was saved!"

The delivered preacher almost tripped over himself in his hurry to get off the ladder to tell his wife.

"Anna, I'm saved! I'm saved!" he called excitedly. Neither she nor any of the other members of his family had fully known of his spiritual struggles.

Then and there his partner and the mother of his children became his first convert as he explained to her the simple way of salvation — by grace through faith in Christ's accomplished work.

Before he had come to trust in salvation by faith, Overholtzer had worried about such a truth causing encouragement of laxity in living. But in his experience, he found the opposite to be true. "When I really knew that I was saved and that God was good enough to save me instantly and without merit on my part, I was overwhelmed by a sense of gratitude that has never left me. It has seemed to me utterly unthinkable that I should not do my utmost to obey Christ who has set me free.

"The Holy Spirit soon taught me that all my prior service had been superficial. I had never given my life to God in full once-for-all consecration, that He might take it and plan it in His own way forever. This I now fully did as the 'reasonable service' of a saved soul. It resulted in new blessings through the Holy Spirit's power and also God's work of 'pruning' to bring about fruitfulness" (John 15: 1, 2).

Doubts sometimes came to tempt the released preacher, but he would immediately repeat the texts he had etched deeply in his mind. "By following this procedure," he said, "it was not long before I ceased doubting forever and full assurance was mine."

The quarantine over, a new Overholtzer returned to preach in the little country church. God blessed his ministry. Opposition resulted in new opportunities for God to manifest His presence.

"In private and in public it was a delight to explain the way of salvation, and many were eager to hear," he noted.

Soon one young man accepted the saving truth. Then another. And another, till there were four. "What a joy," he said, "to follow these first four and to see the Gospel of grace prove itself true in experience." Among these was Ferdy, the young Portuguese who thought that Protestants worship the devil.

A step had been taken on a new path by the young preacher-farmer. It would land him far and wide in the proclamation of this message of salvation without works.

But he had a big hurdle to face: his church denomination. Rules that he himself had helped to draft now turned against him!

What will the elders say? How will my denomination react?

Brother Jesse hadn't long to wait for his answer.

"Brother Jesse!" one man cried. "Do you or do you not still believe in salvation by grace alone?"

8

Here I Stand!

Preacher Overholtzer was required by his denomination to wear a beard and a plain coat without a collar. Once he considered the garb an assist in "keeping saved." Now he felt it was a hindrance in getting his message to those who needed it.

A resolution began forming in his mind. One day when his horse and surrey carried him out the lane toward town the resolution had turned from thought to action. He was gone for several hours, but his family didn't know where. Suddenly a horse and surrey just like theirs stopped in front of the house. A clean-shaven man poked his head out and asked with a twinkle in his eye, "Does Mr. Overholtzer live here?"

His daughter Ruth shyly looked over the stranger. "I think *you* are Mr. Overholtzer."

And he was. He had a new faith and a new face.

That night Overholtzer attended the Farm Bureau Association meeting at the schoolhouse. "I sat near the rear of the crowded auditorium and only later when I rose to discuss a subject before the group did my neighbors recognize me. The excitement of seeing the over-strict minister with his beard removed caused the meeting to break up!

"As a result of that appearance, more curious neighbors came to church and many were saved."

Soon the entire community had heard the news. So many came to hear him preach that the congregation moved to the larger facilities of the elementary schoolhouse. This increased the size of his audience because many unbelievers would come to a neutral auditorium who would not enter the denominational sanctuary.

Driven by new zeal, he tried to visit every home in his rural parish. Many in the community received the truths that had unshackled him, finding freedom and peace in Christ.

"I brought in ministers of other denominations sound in the faith to preach for us — an unheard of thing [in his church] prior to this time. I called on the leading citizens who were not Christians and talked to them about their souls. I mailed out tracts repeatedly to every family over a large area."

He soon became a counselor for the local district of the Christian Endeavor Association and entered into other interdenominational pursuits.

His peace of heart shone out to the community in acts of helpful kindness. Overholtzer's ranch was near the Sacramento River, which overflowed its banks each winter. High levees had been built by the county to keep these waters from flooding the countryside, ruining the crops, damaging the farm buildings and drowning the stock. At times of very high water, all the neighbors systematically watched the levees to detect and repair any small hole or break.

Up until this time Overholtzer would join them during the week, but when Saturday midnight came he would immediately lay down his tools and go home — no matter how great the danger.

"If my salvation depends upon my good works," he had taught, *"I must keep Sunday punctiliously!"*

During his first winter as a "new man," the river began to rise — higher this time than usual. By Sunday the levees were in great danger of breaking. Instead of going home before Sunday dawned, Overholtzer continued on guard with his neighbors.

"News of this simple act spread like wildfire. Men began coming to church who had never been there before — many out of appreciation for my standing with them."

The plain clothing was the next "wood" that he pruned from the tree of his new life. "The distinctive garb often kept strangers aloof as I tried to converse with them. I decided the time had come to remove this also."

The popular preacher was appointed to give the keynote address at the two annual gatherings of the Brethren. For his text for the first sermon, he used Ephesians 2:8 and 9, two of the verses that had shown him the truth that salvation is a free gift.

"My message fell like a bombshell on the audience. Such teaching had never been given in my denomination. Since I had been elected the presiding officer of the conference, the effect was tremendous. The Holy Spirit moved mightily."

Several months elapsed before the second state-wide gathering convened. Church leaders from far and near came to hear Brother Jesse's "heretical" doctrines expounded.

"Leaders kept asking me questions from the floor," he said. "Soon the opposition burst and was not long in resulting in my being brought to trial for preaching salvation by grace."

Under the Brethren form of government, Overholtzer had to be tried by a court made up of all the ordained ministers in the entire state. This meeting they arranged on the spot.

Brother Jesse knew that gifted church leaders would ask questions he couldn't answer at his trial. "The Bible was a new book to me," he declared. "I didn't know all of the ramifications of the doctrine of salvation by grace. But I did know that I was saved and that moment by moment the Holy Spirit was my comforter."

As he faced his dilemma in prayer, a verse he had often read seized his mind: ". . . take no thought beforehand what ye shall speak, neither do ye premeditate: but whatsoever shall be given you in that hour, that speak ye: for it is not ye that speak, but the Holy Ghost."[1] Preacher Overholtzer decided to take that verse literally as he prepared for the confrontation.

For four solid hours he was plied with questions in an effort to refute the teaching of salvation by grace or to tangle him up in this teaching and show that it contradicted other parts of the Scriptures. "The whole Bible was covered by the questions. Numbers of times when a question was being asked I did not have the slightest idea of how to answer it; but in every instance the answer was given me at the moment needed. I marveled that at such times these keen leaders were left speechless. I never learned so much Bible truth in such a short time! Sitting as a court, the decision was that I must give up this teaching, or be deposed from the ministry. I was given one year to think it over."

Like Martin Luther, J. Irvin Overholtzer did not want to leave his church. He wanted to win his brothers to his convictions so they could share his joy. But they were

---
[1] Mark 13:11

equally determined to convince him that he should give up his teaching and remain in good standing with the church.

Twelve months passed slowly. Brother Jesse was often visited by fellow ministers who tried to deter him from his new beliefs. Each one turned sadly away, failing in the purpose for which he had come.

And now the time came for the reckoning.

"Brother Jesse!" cried one of the men at his second trial. "Do you or do you not still believe in salvation by grace alone?"

"I believe it more strongly than ever!" he replied. "The events of the past year convince me that God's blessing is upon this teaching."

Young Portuguese Ferdy Custer was in the group at the trial. As his boss was being grilled, the teen-ager became exasperated at the questioners. Suddenly he leaped to his feet and blurted out: "Who are you trying to glorify, the church or the Lord?"

Mr. O asked him to please sit down and not get involved. As Custer later reconstructed the event he remembered that Mr. O never raised his voice during the trial or became angry. He answered each question calmly and confidently with very little evidence of emotion.

The Brethren leaders launched into another concerted effort to show him he was wrong. Again Overholtzer experienced what he called a "miracle of the Lord" by replying instantly with answers to questions he was not of himself prepared to answer.

And then another "bomb" fell on the confused and excited Brethren. A mature, gifted pastor from Fresno stood up and faced the group. "If you are going to try Brother Jesse," he said, "you can try me, too, for I believe it also!"

The ministers were shocked into silence. And then each tried to speak first. In all the bedlam, no decision was reached. Overholtzer reluctantly made his own decision to part with the Brethren. He was never officially relieved of his title.

Sad at the parting from his friends, Overholtzer hitched his team and drove slowly back to his farm. That night he studied late, pondering again the issues that had shattered his ecclesiastical world. He recited again the verses that had brought the light and prayed as he looked down the long, long road ahead.

But the peace he had received — assurance of salvation by grace alone — was as firm as a rock.

Spurgeon, you are utterly wrong! A child of five cannot possibly savingly believe!

9

Knicker and Pigtail Experiment

Mr. O stared in unbelief at the page in front of him. Spread out on his desk was a volume from a set of twenty-four written by Charles Haddon Spurgeon, famed British preacher in London, of an earlier generation. The farmer reveled in its message, "for every single sermon explained the way of salvation by grace through faith."

But now, as he was underlining his way through one of Spurgeon's sermons, he was startled to read: "A child of five, if properly instructed, can as readily believe and be regenerated as anyone."

Overholtzer let the book fall on the desk. *Spurgeon*, he said to himself, *you are utterly wrong. A child of five cannot possibly savingly believe.* Dismissing the matter, he went on with his reading. But he couldn't forget the amazing statement.

It haunted him the following day as he went about his work. *A child of five . . . if properly instructed . . . can as readily believe and be regenerated as anyone. . . . That just can't be. That just can't be,* he said to himself, completely unconvinced.

Admiration that he had for the great theologue, his mind kept going back again and again to those shocking words.

Finally he decided to stage an experiment. "I did not have the faith to try *five*-year-old children," he said, "so I looked for an opportunity to explain the way of salvation to children *nine* or *ten years* of age. That was going a long way for me in those days, for I had never known a child even of that early age to be born again."

He did not begin with any of his own brood or with any children in the families of his church. "I didn't want them to know what I was doing," he said. "I knew they would oppose it. We had quite a number of children in Sunday school from non-Christian homes. I decided to experiment with these. If I couldn't help them, I probably would not hurt them either."

He waited for an opportunity to speak in private to some of these children. One day it came.

"Sonny, may I speak to you for a minute?" he asked.

"Sure!" the lad replied.

Carefully the preacher explained the way of salvation to the nine year old, then asked him if he would like to receive Christ as his personal Saviour. He was somewhat surprised when the boy readily knelt and opened his heart to Jesus Christ.

Ten-year-old Ruby was next. She knew Mr. Overholtzer as a pastor in her local community. One day when his path crossed hers he asked her if she was a Christian.

"I don't know," Ruby replied.

"Are you saved?" he asked, but again she said she didn't know.

"How do we get saved?" he persisted.

"By being good," she answered.

"How good do you have to be?"

"You have to be awful good."

"How 'awful' good?"

"You have to be awful, *awful* good!" she replied.

"Are you that good?"

"No."

"Well," he answered, "I guess you are not saved then." Looking at the perplexed little girl he said, "I'm not that good either!"

This was too much for Ruby.

Her eyes got big with wonder as much as to say: *If you're not that good, then you're not saved. Who then can be saved?*

With great earnestness she asked, "How then do you get saved?"

"What a joy it was," Overholtzer related, "to explain God's plan of salvation through the finished work of Christ on the cross."

Ruby readily received Christ.

The new children's evangelist asked each little convert not to tell anyone. If the experiment were to fail, Mr. O reasoned, the fewer who knew, the better.

In a short time some twenty children had received Christ. One little girl refused for a time because her grandfather had told her she could not be saved until she had been baptized with water. But after two or three conversations she, too, accepted Christ.

Mr. O watched his little experiments closely — critically. Among his pigtail conferees were two little sisters aged nine and eleven. Their father was an infidel, and their mother had not been to church in all the nine years they had lived in that community.

During this period Overholtzer, liberated from the works-oriented teaching of his denomination, was instrumental in uniting his church and four others of his new persuasion in evangelistic services. A tent was set up on a corner of a grain field. The Irish evangelist W. P. Nicholson, of the Bible Institute of Los Angeles, was engaged to preach. To the amazement of Mr. O, the mother of these two girls attended the opening service.

At the first invitation the mother stepped forward and accepted Christ as Saviour.

"I wondered what had influenced her to come," Overholtzer recalled, "for all of our efforts to win her previously had been of no avail. I decided to ask why."

Her reply shook from him any doubts he had held about the credibility of conversions among little children.

"I came," she replied, "because of the changed lives of my two little girls."

"If little girls, dealt with in secret and even forbidden to publicly confess Christ, could give evidence of salvation," Overholtzer declared, "then child evangelism is real and Spurgeon was right."

The reply of the mother of those little girls was like the voice of God guiding him into a new and exciting ministry.

Now the preacher-farmer faced a harvest so vast, a resource so rich and a strategy so simple that he needed time to plan his next move. He also needed time for prayer, but the thin walls of his frame house where nine active children were at play offered no seclusion for quiet meditation. Besides, the Overholtzers rose at five to begin a busy day on the farm, and they worked until dark.

"I had built a tiny room on the front porch for study and prayer," he said, "and I now arose at 4:00 A.M. to spend an hour with the Lord before the family was astir. But I soon found that I had physical limitations — even when the spirit was willing. I often fell asleep on my knees."

The farm had a windbreak of four rows of eucalyptus

trees extending for a quarter of a mile from the house. These trees had dense foliage. Again and again Mr. O sought their seclusion as a "prayer closet." Many a spiritual battle was fought there, many a blessing captured. Many an illumination cast light on an uncertain path, and many an answered prayer was first uttered there in the trees he had planted on barren ground years before.

One evening as Overholtzer sat reading a book by the seventeenth-century theologian George Fox, founder of the Quaker movement, he was gripped by the author's assertion that a spiritual Christian ought to "light up" at least two counties.

"This I undertook to do," Mr. O recorded. "My church paid me no salary and I had to work my farm as a means of livelihood. I soon realized that I was constantly overworking. But I reasoned that since I was doing this for the Lord He would sustain me. I learned, however, that when we flagrantly break the laws of nature, God will not work a miracle to deliver us from the penalty."

In Overholtzer's case, the penalty was severe. Hard work, little sleep, concern over family responsibilities pushed him into a complete nervous collapse. It occurred at the height of the 1918 flu epidemic and seemed in part to stem from a bad case of the dreadful disease.

His daughter Ruth, studying that year at the Bible Institute of Los Angeles, heard from friends that her father was so sick they feared he would not recover.

But God spared the man who was to look back upon the trial as a blessing. As Mr. O lay on his bed "looking up," the Lord opened the Scriptures to him. By night and by day, for hours at a time, one passage after another would be illumined by the Holy Spirit. He later referred to this experience as his "theological seminary."

"I knew many passages by heart, so the Lord threw light on passage after passage without my having strength to read. I look back upon those weeks as the most fruitful in my whole life."

His only hope of recovery, the doctor advised, was to move from the farm to the coast. "Even then," the physician warned, "you must not resume public work for at least a year."

It was both a beginning and an end. Since the knicker and pigtail experiment had worked, there was nothing else to consider but hanging up the hoe and giving all to an evangelistic outreach to the children of the world.

Ahead lay many tests of endurance for the sturdy German farmer and his devoted family. But God had called. There was no thought of turning back.

Lord, I am willing to be used or abused that Thou might be glorified!

10

To the Busy Haunts of Men

Patience now became an ingredient in the cup which the pioneer had to drink.

God had called him to a new work; the doctor had ordered him off the farm; borrowed money had to be paid back; yet he lay flat on his back, unable to answer the challenges he faced.

A "For Sale" sign was posted on the ranch, and the whole family watched for the dramatic answer to prayer that was sure to come. To Mrs. Overholtzer and the children it was a daring venture. To Mr. O it was neither daring nor soon enough.

"I made several inquiries in San Francisco about where I might work and found that my volunteer services would be welcomed by a 'very spiritual' organization," he said. "Since no remuneration was offered I made no move to go. I realize now that I should have launched out by faith, but I had not yet learned how to trust God for daily bread for a big family with no *visible* means of support."

The sale of the farm was not made until after the family had moved to the city. Excitedly, they began packing for their move to Berkeley in 1919. Gathering his strength, Mr. O made a trip to San Francisco to search for a house which would accommodate his large family. As his father had before him, J. Irvin Overholtzer wanted his children to receive a good education. He also wanted them to have the advantage of being under the ministry of Dr. Lapsley A. McAfee, pastor of Berkeley's First Presbyterian Church.

Mr. O chose a house near Dr. McAfee's church, 2119 Carlton Street in Berkeley, about a mile south of the University of California campus.

"Coming from the country," Ruth recalls, "we children were intrigued by the sliding doors. These doors separated the hall from the living room and the living room from the dining room.

"There were four bedrooms and a 'cubby hole' that became one of the boys' sleeping area.

"On holidays, Dad would spend all day with us playing games. We loved it!"

Here the preacher slowly recovered from his breakdown that had kept him in bed for many months.

While the glow of health was returning, Overholtzer visited many churches in the San Francisco Bay area to survey the possibilities of engaging in evangelism among children.

"It was apparent that the unsaved were not coming to church," he said. "In Oakland I discovered that if only one-seventh of the people in that city would decide to go to church on any given Sunday there would not be room for even that many in the existing churches.

"It became clear to me that if we were to win the unsaved — especially the children — we must develop some plan or program to reach the unsaved *outside* the church buildings first, and then bring them into the congregation."

Further, he found that only a small percentage of children were attending *any* Sunday school.

"A great burden came upon me for these unreached boys and girls," he wrote, "especially in the Bay cities of California, where a million people lived. Beginning in Judaea, I longed to encompass the world with an outreach for children." While recuperating, he did some personal evangelism.

One day in San Francisco's Golden Gate Park he met a manly little fellow who wanted him to buy a pencil. "It's only five cents," the boy quickly added.

"No, I don't need a pencil but here is five cents. I'll just give it to you."

The little boy refused. He wouldn't take the nickel until his "customer" had taken the pencil.

Then Mr. O asked, "Do you know about Jesus and God?"

"Yes," the little salesman replied. "I read about them in the *Sunday Examiner*."

"Do you go to Sunday school?"

"No, but before we moved I used to go to a *Friendly Indian Club*."

Mr. O sat down on a bench. "Would you like to have me tell you about Jesus and God?"

"Sure!" came the reply. He looked at his watch. "I have fifteen minutes."

The children's evangelist started at the beginning and told him the story of salvation. Never had he encountered a more attentive audience. The boy forgot all about his "fifteen minutes" and eagerly accepted Christ as his personal Saviour.

Six months passed. Restless to preach again, Overholtzer

accepted an invitation to teach a Bible class at the Berkeley First Presbyterian Church. His class grew rapidly and other calls began opening up new opportunities to teach the Scriptures. He was urged to accept ordination but chose rather to work as a layman.

As Mr. Overholtzer maintained a widening circle of Bible classes, he carefully continued to lay plans for an evangelistic outreach to children.

A realtor in Oakland, recalling the days when he sat in Mr. O's Bible classes, says he was "gripped and held" by the clear Bible messages. "My wife and I were active in our church and had served for twenty-five years. But we had never heard anyone open up the Scriptures like Mr. Overholtzer. He had been unmistakably given a revelation of deep truths in God's Word and had the ability to reveal them to others. He also was blessed with faith that eventually overcame every doubt, criticism, failure and trial. He knew he was doing God's will, and that God was with him — no matter what men thought, said or did! Also, Mr. Overholtzer had vision and discernment. He dreamed of an army of evangelists to children circling the globe at a time when it seemed impossible to us, and doubtless to others also."

In homes, churches, halls — even on the campus of the University of California — J. Irvin Overholtzer presented the marvels of God's Word to eager audiences. Always he talked of the needy and responsive field of children, telling how he came to see the truth of child evangelism.

One day in Wheeler Hall at the university, where he was teaching a regular noon Bible class of about a hundred students, he related the story of his knicker and pigtail experiment. He told of the two little girls, daughters of the infidel, whom he had led to Christ. When he had finished, a young woman stood up.

"I was one of those little girls!" she exclaimed. And then she told a fascinated teacher and class her story.

"Actually, I was not one of these two, but I was among the children you first led to Christ," she said.

"You had a hard time getting me to accept Christ. I was an orphan girl and lived with my uncle and grandfather. You told me that all I had to do to be saved was to truly believe on the Lord Jesus, but my grandfather and uncle said I had to be baptized first. You said I could accept Christ and He would save me," she continued, "and that I could be baptized afterwards. And you finally convinced me and I accepted Christ about the same time as the two little girls you were telling about.

"You told me not to tell anybody, but, if you remember, our farm joined the farm of those two other little girls and we told each other. For a whole year our playtime was spent in playing church and Sunday school and reading our Bibles together."

That girl later entered full-time Christian work. "It was another prod from the Lord," said Mr. O, "to spur me on in establishing child evangelism."

He looked for opportunities to lay his life on the line in humble service. "Lord," he cried with deep heart earnestness, "I am willing to be used or abused that Thou might be glorified!"

That prayer must have been heard in Heaven. The pioneer of child evangelism would have to be a sturdy soul who could withstand discouragement and endure privation.

We had never heard of such results in evangelistic work with so little effort and cost. Our enthusiasm for child evangelism was boundless.

11

Unfolding Vision

For three years Mr. O taught his Bible classes. He also worked in a downtown San Francisco rescue mission, all the while watching and praying for a plan to implement his burden for unreached children.

Most of the children who attended Sunday school those days were not being won to Christ. Dr. Clarence H. Benson, director for Christian education at Moody Bible Institute, Chicago, stated that only twenty percent were actually being led to Christ in this field pregnant with evangelistic potential.

And there were the literally oceans of children beyond the walls of the church buildings.

Overholtzer was not one to get his direction from man.

He had learned the way, back there on the ranch, under the eucalyptus trees. God always had a plan. It was his to find it.

His students joined him in prayer.

There were five classes of children he hoped to reach: those completely outside the church; those in liberal Sunday schools; those of other faiths and cults; isolated foreign or minority groups; and unsaved in evangelical churches.

"To attempt to reach the children of these various classes through a denominational setup would utterly fail," observed Overholtzer.

God gave the key: Make the work interdenominational!

"We did not want to interfere with the Sunday schools. Instead, we wanted to do everything possible to build them up. It seemed that the Lord showed me His plan. This was to start interdenominationally slanted weekday Bible classes for children. These classes would meet in Christian homes after school. The weekday hour in a home, I reasoned, might get past some of the prejudice and indifference which I knew existed among parents of children who were attending no Sunday school."

The children's evangelist watched warmly as students and housewives moved onto the scene, into neglected tenement areas, into minority group sections, into isolated places — holding classes, winning boys and girls to Christ and teaching them the Word of God. Even from the first there were glowing reports of the salvation of many children.

The Sacramento Valley fruit-grower was jubilant!

This was *real* and *eternal* fruit-gathering.

And what a crop!

"We had never heard of such results in evangelistic work," he said, "with so little effort and cost."

But the teachers must have lessons. There were none on the market geared for weekday evangelism and Bible study for children. These Mr. O undertook to write, first having them mimeographed and later printed. "Faulty" and "crude" he described them, but "we were learning."

And the teachers needed training!

Overholtzer set up a training school for them. He conducted it in the morning hours, five days a week. Here courses were taught in Bible doctrine as well as in methods for reaching and teaching the boys and girls. Teachers also demonstrated how to use their simple homemade visual aids in clarifying to children the great doctrines of the Bible.

The blessing and know-how of winning children overflowed to the Sunday schools. Teachers who had learned how to evangelize, won boys and girls in their Sunday schools. Nearly every evangelical church in the Bay area was touched. In even liberal churches some were permitted to hold what they called "decision" services.

The responsibility of providing for his large family, carrying on his adult Bible classes, the demands of the mission, plus the burden of developing the program of child evangelism could have been emotionally shattering. But Mr. O had learned through one nervous collapse that God's work run according to God's direction will have His supply. One's own overheated concern made it move neither smoother nor faster.

He worked hard and slept well, buoyed by the assurance that the time for launching a program to reach children for Christ had come. He pictured it sweeping the world, harvesting a mighty crop of children for Christ.

Mr. O took a shirt-sleeves approach to his work. What he asked of his associates he first demanded of himself. On a scrap of paper still in his files he had written: "Faith is dead to doubt, dumb to discouragement and blind to impossibility."

A niece from Los Angeles who spent many of her teen-age summers with the Overholtzers recalls how completely her uncle relied on the Lord for the smallest provision.

One day while returning from a shopping trip Vera Billheimer stopped in front of a meat market, "not knowing why." After buying two dozen pork chops, she hurried home. Aunt Anna was in a quandary. Uncle Jesse had brought home a distinguished friend of the mission and there was no meat for dinner! Vera's pork chops saved the day. When informed about the brush with embarrassment, Mr. O said matter-of-factly, "The Lord has never failed us."

In the city of Oakland a young Plymouth Brethren man by the name of Harry A. Ironside operated a religious supply depot called "Western Book and Tract Store." One of his suppliers was Pickering and Ingles, Brethren publishing house in England.

Probably on some casual visit, though no one knows exactly when or how, one of the children's workers noticed a little book of colors in the materials on display. "For telling the Gospel story," some sales person no doubt advised. *Ah!* thought the worker, *this I can use.*

All of a sudden there was a run on the little book known as "The Wordless Book." It has been used by the multiplied thousands since, pointing, in the universal language of color, multitudes of children to Christ.

Later Mr. O, in reaffirming his call to child evangelism, in the city of Chicago, would use it with child after child in five hot weeks of open-air work in that city. His diary records that through its use there were more than five thousand decisions for Christ among the children.

Overholtzer was not without his critics as he began the work of reaching the children there in Berkeley.

You mean that these child evangelism people are talking to youngsters and pretending to believe they are saved?

Children! Will they hold out?

And they had criticism for his not seeking secular employment to support his large family. Time and again the exchequer was very low.

In answer to the first criticism he said: "One who catches the vision for this work must throw himself upon the Holy Spirit's ministry in bringing souls to conviction, to repentance, to saving faith and regeneration. Unless you depend wholly on God rather than on self, you will utterly fail in practical results. Christ talked about the little ones which believe in me (Matthew 18:6). What else could He have meant except that a child can savingly believe?" And Mr. O had his own experiences to prove it.

For the second criticism God met him in an incident that for him would forever silence his oppressors.

It was a critical time for the crusader. The organization had as yet not been formed. There was no committee. There were no good friends of the work. There was no salary. There were no regular givers. There was God, His call, a family of eleven and meager resources.

Would God provide?

"Many said it was folly," he wrote. "It was facing abject want." More, it was whispered that it was wrong, for the family was dependent upon the parent — the breadwinner. If the parent would bring suffering upon himself, that was not so bad, but what would become of the children? Was it not sinful to involve them in another's folly?

"But in prayer the die was cast, and truly the resources did grow less. All hell seemed to conspire to destroy even what resources there were.

"Soon the last available dollar was in sight, then it was partly spent. Did God know? Had He forsaken? Would He really provide? No one knew how acute was the need except some of the home circle.

"Should not some employment be sought?

"Would it not be best to borrow from a friend?

"If God was going to answer prayer, why was He so slow?

"Satan stormed the castle of faith with these and many other questions."

Then there was a phone call from San Francisco with a

request for an interview. It would take some of the precious "less than a dollar" to pay carfare.

Should the word be given to go to the interview? The person hadn't even intimated what the purpose of the interview was.

"The still small voice said 'Go,'" related Mr. Overholtzer. And go he did.

The friend had a gift for him in the way of a one-thousand-dollar government bond! And he told Mr. O where it could be immediately cashed. "God has been talking to me," the man said. "Use it for yourself."

"There have been hundreds of miracles since," said the tempted and tried Christian worker, "but this one will always remain unique; it answered once for all the questions that Satan and well-meaning friends had raised."

Overholtzer needed that lesson. It would encourage him many and many a time in the difficult days to come as he moved out from Berkeley to begin a school for training children's workers in Chicago during the time that came to be called the Great Depression.

It seemed the height of folly, yet I was obedient to what I believed to be the leading of the Lord.

12

Chicago Crucible

The lonely sound of a whistle drifted over the prairie as the Chicago express highballed through the night, racing toward the sunrise and the bustling city on the lake.

From the window of his coach, Mr. O gazed out on the moonlit country where, exactly sixty-nine years earlier, in June, 1864, his father was on the dangerous trail with covered wagon, heading west for the sake of God and conscience. Now his seventh son was traveling the opposite way, making another trip, in obedience to God for the spiritual welfare of children.

The train shot past the west-side tenements, dived with a roar under the bridges of the commercial district. Then, hissing proudly, it came to a halt at Union Station.

Few took notice of the ordinary-looking man who disembarked that hot June day in 1933. Chicago was caught up in the Second World's Fair, the "Century of Progress Exposition," that would enroll 22,317,221 people between May 27 and November 12 that year.

Prohibition had come to an end in 1933 after the banning of alcoholic beverages for thirteen years. Adolph Hitler had become dictator of Germany. Wiley Post was hailed by wild cheers after flying around the world in seven days, eighteen hours and forty-nine minutes.

Mr. O bought a paper and studied the long columns of real-estate ads. Where should he look for suitable quarters to live and to begin a school? He folded the paper, breathed a prayer and started out.

How splendid did pioneer work appear! He had big plans and high hopes for great accomplishments. Was not his call to the world? Chicago, Mr. O considered, was but the next step out.

Oppressive heat bore down on the children's evangelist as he walked the streets of the strange city. His steps naturally led him to the northern part, near the great Moody Church founded by the man whose writings had been used of God to bring him spiritual light.

How long ago that seemed! How grateful he was as he thought of his deliverance. And now he rejoiced that he was on a mission to bring this message of salvation to the children.

As he walked, in his heart he sang (he couldn't carry a tune except, as he said, "in a basket"): "To the work, to the work! Let us do with our might what our hands find to do!"

Little did Mr. O realize what a full measure God had for him — of testing and blessing — in this big city, so far from home.

The city was sizzling in a heat wave. July 9 found him writing home, still without a suitable site for his prospective school. He redoubled his efforts, at the same time visiting churches and inviting laymen to the school which he scheduled to open in September.

On July 19 he notified his faithful followers at home that he had secured a house with rooms to sublet. He moved into one of the rooms and prayed for others to come to help pay the rent on the entire complex.

By July 24 he recorded in his diary that he had twenty-six cents in his pocket and a discouraging number of prospects for his school. But, undaunted, his song for the day was the doxology. His verse: "Thanks be unto God who always causeth us to triumph in Christ."

Closer and closer the opening of school came. Harder and harder he pressed on. Small gifts trickled in from his California friends, but he was kept perpetually at the point of need.

In August, with no money to pay, he saw the gas turned off in his house.

Only one roomer came to share the rent when the school opened. The rest of the handful of students lived at home.

The success the indomitable children's crusader had envisioned for his coveted school in America's second city, with its heavy child population, didn't come. Not only were the students few, but those who came had real difficulties in leading children to the Lord.

He closed his first session early in the spring and determined to push through the work of reaching boys and girls in the Windy City. He would go out on the streets himself to contact them.

Successful though he was, he became physically and mentally exhausted by summer's end. And his plans to reopen the school collapsed.

What was the answer? Why had this school for which he felt the Lord had so signally burdened him failed?

There were two or three minor doctrines which Mr. Overholtzer believed and taught that he soon found were not believed by leading evangelicals. "As time went on," he later told, "this brought opposition to the work by some of our spiritual leaders."

A number of those who shared these beliefs which he had taught in the Berkeley school urged him to start a new denomination. But this couldn't be, reasoned Overholtzer. "Such a step would have thwarted the whole purpose of my call to child evangelism which, it was clear, was to be carried on interdenominationally."

Characteristically, he decided to study the Word for himself and find the answers. "I asked the Lord to show me the truth in His Word and promised Him I would be true to *whatever He showed me, at whatever cost.*"

He completely shut himself apart from the public and proceeded to restudy the Bible.

"I outlined in a word-by-word study most of the New Testament books," he later wrote.

Months were spent in this way. He gave his entire time to study and prayer.

"Bit by bit I became convinced that the doctrines in question were erroneous," he said. And the Lord was dealing with his attitude as well as his beliefs. In his diary he recorded, "I see clearly what folly it is to voice an opinion (hardly worthwhile even to hold it) in regard to the interpretation of some Scripture that deals with only minor questions. . . . I was overwhelmed with humility and surrendered my pride of opinion, which I did not realize I so terribly had."

The day came that cold winter in Chicago when Mr. O arose at dawn, washed and shaved, and then spent a long time on his knees. After a simple breakfast, he took a long look at some of the thirty booklets he had written and had used as texts in the Berkeley school. Tears fell as he thought of the past and his mistakes. . . . But this was no time for regrets. He had seen his errors. There was only one thing to do.

"It was at the height of the Depression," wrote Mr. O. "Banks were closing and soup lines were lengthening. I sorely needed the money from the sale of my books to continue the work."

But he had made a sacred promise — and he kept it. He burned every book in stock.

"How great was the blessing that immediately followed," he said. Christian leaders, one after another, accepted his confession at face value and immediately gave him their moral support. He published a retraction in a four-page tract entitled "That the Lord Jesus Christ Might Be Glorified."

Another peak in the hurdles of Chicago had been passed.

He wrote letters to personal friends asking their forgiveness and urged anyone who could enlighten him about any further errors to do so at once!

As a seal of divine approval Mr. O asked the Lord to renew his call so he would know "beyond a peradventure that my call to child evangelism was of the Lord and still in force."

One day not long after this plea, God met him.

"As I was praying," he said, "the spirit of prayer came upon me as I had never known it. While fully conscious, I seemed to lose the sense of time or place. For hours I literally lay on the floor on my face and wept as the Spirit *compelled* me to pray for the salvation of the children. In great agony I was led to pray from country to country for the children of that country.

"This continued until I had covered all of the countries of the world except Russia. I was just as burdened to pray for the children of Russia but could not bring myself to pray for them. Then the burden lifted."

About three weeks later the experience was repeated.

"Again I prayed for the children, country by country, until I came to Russia. I felt I *must* pray for the children of that great country. In fact, it seemed I would die if I did not! Yet the agony was so great it seemed I would die if I *did* pray for them. I told the Lord I was willing to die then and there if He would give me the strength and faith to pray for the salvation of Russia's children. He gave enabling grace and the prayer was uttered. Then the burden lifted." Mr. O was satisfied. Yes, the Lord had miraculously renewed his call.

But still another issue had to be settled. "While I found the teaching of the Scripture clear and ample that children could and should be evangelized, I had not yet found a text that clearly taught that they could and would be *born again* if they believed." Again he sought his answer in God's Word.

"I was busily outlining the Book of Ephesians," he said, "when the light burst upon me that the Epistle was addressed to the 'saints which are at Ephesus'; yet in chapter six, verses one and two, the apostle spoke directly to children of believing parents. This clearly taught that such children had been born again, for 'saints' surely are!"

Overholtzer said, "This not only proved that children could be and are born again, but that evidently child evangelism was the common practice in the families of the believers at Ephesus! I searched the other Epistles and found the same thing in Colossians 1:2 and 3:20."

After discovering this truth, Overholtzer checked with Dr. H. A. Ironside, then pastor of Moody Church. "Is my interpretation correct?" he asked him. "It most assuredly is," Dr. Ironside replied.

But the Chicago crucible, which was to be the symbol of testing and ultimate triumph for the children's evangelist, was not yet full. A strong-willed, independent Pennsylvania Dutchman, brought up on a do-it-yourself policy in things secular and spiritual, Jesse Overholtzer had had a hard time coming to trust in Christ *by grace alone* for salvation. He now had yet to see that *victory* in the Christian life — over sin and for service — was also a matter of grace.

There were still many trying days in his cheap little room in Chicago. Sometimes he was defeated . . . sometimes victorious.

Could this roller-coaster experience be the norm for Christian living?

On January 2 he wrote in his diary, "Never knew such agony of spirit in prayer as this morning. Felt so wicked and vile in myself. . . ."

January 29: "Today I placed on the altar all legitimate pleasures of life and health, if these things should need to be given up for God's glory or for the furtherance of His cause."

Still the full measure of victory that he sought eluded him. *What was God trying to show him?*

March 14: "I don't know if I can describe my experience with the Lord yesterday morning. I was meditating on love and I began to see myself as I really am — a big hypocrite. I don't love the poor and outcast. I don't love the heathen. I only love the Lord and souls and the Word a very little. I am not unselfish like Jesus was. Ambition and duty and pride have more to do with my service than *love*. I can't love; I am helpless. O God! fill every part of my being with the love of God — not only the 'greatest thing in the world' but the rarest."

All the while the burden of reaching children was upon him. "Had such a battle over discouragement and perplexity about the work," he wrote. Then — the following quotations appear in the diary.

April 14: ". . . thine expectation shall not be cut off" (Proverbs 23:18). "If thou faint in the day of adversity, thy strength is small" (Proverbs 24:10). "For the gifts and calling of God are without repentance" (Romans 11:29). "For the vision is yet for an appointed time, but at the end it shall speak, and not lie; though it tarry, wait for it; because it will surely come, it will not tarry" (Habakkuk 2:3).

Mr. O had been reading articles on victorious Christian

living by Charles G. Trumbull, editor of *The Sunday School Times*. Trumbull had stressed that victory was not something you struggled for. It was by faith — just like salvation — entirely unmerited. *All of grace.* All one had to do was yield one's self fully to Him and trust Him for the victory.

But to Overholtzer this seemed too simple. *Salvation by grace, yes; but not victory in everyday Christian living.*

Just as he had disagreed with Moody on salvation by grace, and Spurgeon over the fact that little children could savingly believe, now he disagreed with Trumbull on Christian victory!

Again he went to the Word to find his answers. And he did all he could in his power to prove his dedication. He was serious with the Lord, willing for anything, regardless of the cost.

On February 25 he wrote: "Last night the spirit of prayer and confession came upon me. I wept and prayed. Made a still further surrender of myself. I don't know what more I can surrender except my nothingness. I'm willing to live or die. To be ill. To undergo any suffering or privation that Jesus might be glorified."

Slowly Overholtzer began to see the lesson: Victory *is* by grace, through faith, just as is justification.

All the striving in the world won't achieve it.

It's simply received, as a gift.

"I see at last that teaching sanctification by works has been one cause of my trouble," he wrote on that significant day of February 10. "God has permitted what has happened to me to *shake* me out of this terrible error." Years later he wrote in his autobiography, "I had not seen the teaching of 'Christ in you' (Colossians 1:27) and that He who indwells each believer will live *His* life of victory in us if we are willing to trust Him to do it . . . 'Christ liveth in me' of Galatians 2:20 is the normal Christian experience. . . . As in justification, we cannot be saved by working or struggling for our salvation, so in victory over sin Jesus must 'do it all'. . . . He will do just that when we yield to Him and trust Him for victory.

"What a struggle it was to give up the old 'works' idea for victory," he wrote further. And in his diary for these crucial days he said, "Had been *trying* to be crucified. . . . Saw I could not do it. I was really crucified with Him when He died. I am to claim it." His last note on this entry was: "Self is such a 'bad egg' and such a nuisance!"

From the time Mr. O saw the truth of victory in Christ — over sin and for service — as a gift of God and not of works, his life took on new confidence and purpose. On March 8 he entered in his diary these significant words: "I have the peace of God and have had it constantly since I took it by faith alone. How terrible it seems that I did not know this long ago."

Out of these experiences came a book entitled *The Victorious or Spirit-filled Life* that has brought blessing to countless others.

For sixteen years Mr. O had tried to "keep justified" by works. Another sixteen years he struggled for victory in Christian living and service. Now he was set free from self-effort to obtain the spiritual blessings and usefulness in service he so longed for. A new day was dawning.

"This," he wrote later, "was the beginning of new blessing and power in all of my ministry."

The Chicago crucible was now full. The dross had been consumed. A vessel meet for the Master's use was ready to be poured out in blessing to the nation . . . the world.

Overholtzer had come to Chicago to set up a school for training others. Instead, God had taken *him* to school. He had learned lessons he would never forget. He would teach them at another school yet to be founded.

It seemed utterly impossible to respond to a worldwide call, unknown as I was and with so little ability for such a task. I decided to begin with one day at a time.

13

Trajectory!

Chill was the wind that swept Chicago streets on the morning of March 27, 1935, as Mr. O stepped out of his north-side room.

His life, arched with changing skies, had taken on a calm assurance. Gone forever was the old "works" idea for victorious living — even for pushing ahead the child evangelism movement. Sealed forever in his heart and mind were two things: the truth that children are *born again* when they truly receive Jesus Christ as Saviour and his call to reach these children worldwide.

Overholtzer's trust in God was deep-seated. He was completely committed to please and obey the One who had called Him.

[93]

He was thrust out onto a broad, exciting road of possibilities. A rugged, ruddy farmer, crying out as a lone voice in a wilderness of neglect. Who would help him? Where should he begin?

Mr. O was walking toward the lake on Chicago Avenue. "Well," he said, addressing the concrete forest, "I'm right here in Chicago. Why not start here? A city of three million people is no more difficult for God than a small town!"

He walked on, praying: "Lord, I need *big* men. I need men with Christian influence to pull the blinders from the eyes of Christians. So many are neglecting the children."

His pace quickened. His heart began to sing there on the streets where Dwight L. Moody — "that deluded evangelist" — had gathered children to tell them about Jesus and His love.

Paul Rood. Dr. Paul Rood! He knows about our work among the children in Northern California. I'll see him.

The appointment made, the crusader was on his way to the two-story brick parsonage of Lakeview Covenant Church. Dr. Paul W. Rood was one of God's "big men."

Even while pulling off his overcoat, Mr. O began relating to Dr. Rood the events of the past few weeks, telling of his renewed call; how he had shrunk from the implications of a global thrust.

Praise filled the room as the two men talked on and on — Paul Rood hunched over his big desk listening; J. Irvin Overholtzer outlining his plan for organizing the new movement.

And then they were on their knees, after being joined by Carlton E. Null, of the Pocket Testament League. Three men in a humble room, noticed only by God, began that morning to feel the power of Heaven come down.

Arise, cry out in the night! The prophet Jeremiah's words in Lamentations 2:19 had often impressed Mr. O. *Pour out thine heart like water before the face of the Lord: lift up thy hands toward him for the life of thy young children, that faint for hunger in the top of every street.*

The burden of prayer ploughed deep, breaking up the natural reserve of the children's crusader. As it had before, his enormous concern moved him to tears. They flowed uncontrolled as he wept and wept in front of these two men. Embarrassed, he tried unsuccessfully to stop weeping, but the trademark of tears was to become a permanent stamp on his ministry. Thousands would see them and feel with him the *must* of the ministry to boys and girls.

To his death, Mr. O could not discuss the plight of unevangelized children or listen to reports of their conversion without moist eyes and wet cheeks.

The prayers came to an end and the men rose from their knees. Light was still filtering through the windows. The concrete forest outside still bustled with the hum of men and machines. "Mr. Overholtzer," Dr. Rood was saying, "I want you to speak at our prayer meeting this week. I want our people to share in the new work."

The faithful streamed into the church that Wednesday evening to hear Mr. O read the eighteenth chapter of Matthew, emphasizing verse fourteen: "It is not the will of your Father . . . that one of these little ones should perish."

Here and there heads nodded agreement. When their pastor opened the meeting for testimonies one man confessed: "I was convicted of sin as a very young lad, but no one would deal with me because they said I was too young." A woman stood to her feet and dabbed her eyes with her handkerchief as she told of the years of sin she could have been spared.

Later, during the summer of 1935, Mr. O was invited to hold "decision services" at Lakeview during vacation Bible school. Pastor Rood found himself caught up in the spirit of the work as he dealt with the stream of youngsters who came to the inquiry room. His face beaming, Dr. Rood recounted to Mr. O the very words of some of the youngsters as they opened their hearts to the Saviour. The memory of this tall, stocky pastor-evangelist and well-known president of the World Fundamentals Association down on his knees praying for the children was one Mr. O would long cherish.

The one-man crusade had now doubled to two. The name of a third was scratched on the sheet of paper Dr. Rood handed to Mr. O in his study: "D. L. Foster — Moody Bible Institute."

Mr. O boarded a trolley, greeted the conductor and paid his fare. Clark Street's noisy traffic was but music in his ears. He was on his way to the very school founded by the world-famous evangelist!

He surveyed the administration building's directory searching for the name of "Foster" and rode the elevator to the department of practical work.

Would it be possible to have the endorsement of this great school? Overholtzer thrilled to think of what would happen to the cause of reaching the children if this "West Point of Christian Service" should respond.

Foster's warm handshake and personal interest buoyed hope until the director of practical work admitted: "Mr. Overholtzer, I'm very much interested in helping you, but I cannot serve on your committee without the approval of the president."

"You can't?"

"No. It's policy."

"Well, then, can we see the president?"

D. L. Foster raised his eyebrows and cocked his head as he reached for the phone.

"Too busy!" came the words from the secretary of Dr. Will Houghton. Foster passed them along to Mr. O who had stood to his feet expecting to hurry over to the other office. He sat down again.

"No, let's go over, Mr. Overholtzer. I want Dr. Houghton to hear your story. I think he'll listen."

The president was cordial but unyielding.

"Nearly every day someone comes to my office seeking

the help of the Moody Bible Institute in some spiritual program," Dr. Houghton explained. "But our own program is so big we can do nothing more." The indomitable visitor pressed him. "Do you mean to tell me, Dr. Houghton, that with only one-third of the children in the United States in any Sunday school that the Moody Bible Institute is not going to do anything about it?"

The head of America's largest Bible institute quickly changed his position. "All right, Mr. Overholtzer. What do you want us to do?"

"I want a member of the Moody staff on our Chicago committee," came Mr. O's forthright reply.

Dr. Houghton turned to the director of practical work who had brought the persistent visitor. "Mr. Foster, you are appointed."

Together the men left, those five words still sounding in their ears. They shook hands warmly. The three-man team was about to become four.

"There's another man you should see here in Chicago," said Foster. "Harry Saulnier. He's director of Christian Endeavor for Greater Chicago."

With the backing of the Moody Bible Institute, could anything be difficult again?

"Hallelujah Harry," man number four, gave Mr. O a ready ear.

Their talk became excited there in the Saulnier living room. It was 1:30 in the morning before they even noticed the time or thought of parting. After "a good prayer meeting," host took guest home.

What mountains of impossibilities were being cast into the sea! The man who only a month ago had barely enough money to buy groceries to stay alive was launching a movement that he hoped would one day circle the globe.

He dared to peg other spiritual leaders of influence. Dr. Harry A. Ironside, serving Chicago's famed Moody Memorial Church, lent his support and commented, "This great Moody

Sunday school believes in and practices child evangelism. In fact, the Moody Church grew out of a Sunday school conducted by D. L. Moody where the children were thoroughly evangelized as children." His associate minister, Dr. Charles A. Porter, was also enlisted. He directed the weeping prophet's path to Frances L. Bennett, the enthusiastic little dynamo who for years had conducted children's meetings for the famed Billy Sunday. In her, Mr. O found enthusiasm for winning children to match his own. "You don't have to convert *me*, Mr. Overholtzer," she exclaimed. "Just tell me what I can do for you!"

Before Overholtzer left her that day, she had literally catapulted the movement nineteen stories up, as well as into Chicago's high society.

"I know just the place for your new committee to meet," Miss Bennett told him. "Mrs. Phillip Armour has a downtown office dedicated to the Lord. She is in Europe at the moment, but I'm certain she would be glad for us to meet there."

And she was! Gwendolin C. Armour, wife of Phillip D. Armour III of the famous Chicago meat-packing family, was a cultured lady of deep Christian commitment. She not only provided office space for the new movement but contributed generously to its work and became the first director for the Chicago chapter.

There was no agenda for that historic first Chicago committee meeting — just one big, burning issue: how to organize a firm base to reach the city's 750,000 unchurched children.

"We must reach them *now*," Mr. O urged in his characteristically quiet but forceful manner. "It is a staggering fact that only one out of every three children in the United States and Canada goes to any Sunday school."

A few days after the collective "amens" of that summer meeting in 1935, Mr. O began gathering together his few belongings and looking homeward. His work in Chicago for the time being was finished. God had blessed his faith far beyond his greatest expectations.

Overholtzer thought of the months of his absence from California and of the reports that had been coming regularly. Factions had chewed at the foundations he had laid in the San Francisco Bay area. Some had withdrawn their support. He was returning now to where his theological mistakes had been made, hoping to reenlist his friends in the work of his renewed call.

Harry Saulnier and George Fasig, two men who had helped Mr. O win children on the streets of Chicago, saw him off. One of them pressed some bills into his hand which helped pay his expenses to California.

The engine of the big bus roared to life. Its wheels began to roll through the concrete forest and west toward the open plains. Mr. O settled back and closed his eyes in prayer.

Along with the call was the clearest command to organize thoroughly for this great undertaking.

14

O is for Organization

Homecoming under other circumstances would have been pure joy. But the farther west Mr. O traveled, the more past failures loomed up to haunt him.

Would that I hadn't been so stubborn when folk tried to show me my error!

Will I be able to regain lost territory in the Bay area for God and the children?

Munching on apples and crackers bought at nearby grocery stores while the other passengers went into the restaurants to eat, Overholtzer had plenty of time for reflection. Through his mind ran a laconic saying of his father's, "The place where you lose a thing is the place to find it."

With forthrightness and candor he determined to face his

mistakes and trust God to be glorified through his attempt to make right everything within his power.

Cool breezes off San Francisco Bay refreshed the weary traveler as he stepped off the bus — home in Berkeley at last. How good it was to see his family who had not been able to be with him. They had known of his sacrifices and shared in them. "I had been called of God," he said, "to launch this new movement at the time when the Depression was at its worst. Two of my young daughters could hardly believe I had not been compelled to call upon relief!"

Far into the night the reunited family shared their experiences of the past months and rejoiced over what God had done.

"My task now," said Overholtzer, "was to organize a child evangelism committee and revive the home Bible classes in the Bay area. Many of such classes were still in operation. Now it was all important to unite them under the larger movement. The cooperation of fundamental pastors was essential."

Here God used his pastor of many years, the Rev. P. M. Walker of the Fruitvale Presbyterian Church, as his go-between. Together they called upon pastors while Mr. O told of how God had shown him his errors there in the Chicago crucible. He told of the men God had brought him in touch with — Harry Ironside, now pastor of Moody Church, and Paul Rood, also well known in the northern California area. He told of their approval of his doctrinal position and their enthusiasm for the new movement for the salvation of children.

Then, with obvious emotion, the evangelist said, "I have burned my teaching books with the errors — every one of them."

The men were impressed.

Overholtzer had changed; of this there was no doubt. What hindered their support of this worthy cause?

In short order the existing home Bible classes were united

with the larger movement. Established "without division," reported Overholtzer, "by the grace of God." He breathed a prayer of thanks.

It was good to be back in his native state — the Golden State of California — with its profusion of flowers and trees he loved so deeply — poinsettias, hibiscus, the fragrant eucalyptus tree and the stately palm.

How good it was to be able to gather flowers in winter! He almost shuddered as he thought of the cold back in Chicago.

But a man with a vision cannot be still. "I felt literally thrust out," he said, "and could not stay anywhere."

In the providence of God, his friend Paul Rood had become elected the new president of the Bible Institute of Los Angeles. In his first year of tenure, Rood inaugurated a new conference to be known as the Torrey Memorial Bible Conference, in tribute to the school's first dean, Dr. Reuben A. Torrey. It was no small honor when one day the children's crusader was asked by the president to share in this historical gathering. "A message on child evangelism. It's needed. I want you to bring it," wrote Dr. Rood.

It would be hard to imagine Mr. O's exultation at this opportunity to present his cause.

The wheels began moving. *If only Rood would consent to head a national committee for the new movement.*

Nothing ever came easy to J. Irvin Overholtzer — his salvation, his being converted to child evangelism, his seeing the truth of Christian victory by grace, the opening and development of the child evangelism work. Every piece of ground was gained by trial. It was so in Los Angeles.

Accepting the invitation to speak at the conference, he immediately made plans to organize a unit with a responsible committee for the Los Angeles area. Christian leaders were cooperative. The Rev. William D. Ogg, assistant pastor of the large Church of the Open Door, gave liberally of his time and advice in the seeking of men for a committee.

After weeks of work, the hour was set for the organizational luncheon. The meal was to cost the amazing amount of twenty-five cents.

But Overholtzer didn't have twenty-five cents!

He and Mrs. Overholtzer were staying in a small apartment near where the luncheon was to be held. With so small a charge for the meal — one arranged at his request for his cause — he started out with an empty pocketbook!

But his faithful God did not forget him. Enroute, lying "face up," waiting for him in a dirty gutter, was a silver coin in the amount of a quarter!

Twice more that day he saw God's provision. Since he was early for the meeting he decided to go back to the apartment for his mail. There was a one-dollar bill in a letter. Then a man sitting next to him at the luncheon insisted on paying for his lunch!

Often Overholtzer met with Dr. Rood in his office for consultation and prayer. Many times their thoughts went back to Chicago and the little prayer meeting in the Lakeview parsonage. Rood's burden for the children was obvious.

If Rood would assume headship of a committee for the national organization now being developed, Overholtzer reasoned, this would mean a great deal in launching the movement nationwide.

February 1 was "O" day, "O" in this case for national organization. Meeting were Rood, Overholtzer and two staff members of the Bible Institute — Carlton E. Null and Cutler B. Whitwell. Two evangelists, Richard Lewis and J. Edwin Orr, in Los Angeles at the time, were invited to participate.

It was probably presumptuous for Overholtzer to think that a man as busy as Paul Rood could become chairman. But his sights were always high. Why not get the best?

Before the meeting Overholtzer had been alone in the little rented apartment while his wife was visiting friends. Incomprehensible as it seems, right under the noses of Christian friends, God had permitted him for two days to be without food.

When the men were getting nowhere trying to elect a head for the committee, Overholtzer felt led to tell of this experience.

Immediately the men reached into their pockets and tried to thrust bills into his hands. But he quickly told them that he didn't need the money, for he had just received a check for one hundred dollars in the mail!

But God used the incident to accomplish His purpose. Overholtzer related, "Immediately the Spirit of God seemed to come upon the meeting in a new way." Dr. Rood said to him, "If you will assume all the routine responsibilities, I am willing to become president of the committee." Dr. Rood continued in this position until he was incapacitated by a stroke in 1952.

Rood's name on the letterhead meant that evangelicals across the country could be assured of the sound evangelical position of the new movement.

He became a real enthusiast for the cause and was later heard to say:

"If I deal with twenty adults, I am usually able to win one to Christ. But if I deal with twenty children, nineteen of them will accept Christ. . . . If I had my life to live over, I would devote it to child evangelism."

One after another important matter of business fell in line. The name of the organization would be Child Evangelism Fellowship. The slogan, suggested by Evangelist Orr: "Capture the Children for Christ."

Cutler Whitwell was elected treasurer.[1] "I thought to myself, *We'll probably hear nothing more of this enthusiast*,"

---

[1] Harry Saulnier shortly became the secretary.

he later remarked, adding "How wrong can one man be?"

Even in those early days the picture impressed on those Mr. Overholtzer enlisted was one of faith in trial, persistence in difficulty and assurance that God would surely use those He touched.

"Dogged determination, indomitable spirit," said Samuel H. Sutherland, then dean of the Bible Institute of Los Angeles, and elected to the local Los Angeles committee. Dr. Sutherland added, "He saw so clearly the job that needed to be done, he assumed everyone else had the same vision. It never occurred to him that anyone would fail. . . ."

They must not.

A whole world of unreached children was at stake.

I seemed driven by the Holy Spirit to visit the cities in the United States and Canada in the least possible time.

15

Man in a Hurry

"There you are, sir," said the pleasant young clerk in the Greyhound bus depot as he stamped two tickets. "The Salt Lake City bus will be leaving from Gate 3."

The man in a hurry thanked him and stuffed the tickets in his coat. He picked up a small valise and joined his wife, waiting quietly in the lobby of the Los Angeles depot.

He touched her shoulder. "I'm so glad you could join me on this trip, Anna," he said warmly.

1936 was hardly the year for a cross-country trip, calling people nationwide to a new program. The country was still in the throes of the Depression.

There were still soup lines. The Works Progress Administration was furnishing special projects to make work for men unable to find jobs. Millions were still on direct relief.

Weather-wise it was a year to be remembered. The winter was one of the coldest, the summer one of the hottest ever to be recorded.

In the spring unprecedented floods in the East caused thousands to be homeless, hundreds to die. During the summer in the Midwest nearly three thousand died in a sizzling heat wave which lasted weeks. In the Western plains rainless skies burned the little foliage remaining. Farmers, too, turned to relief to provide food for their tables, while precious top soil was carried miles away by dust storms.

It was also the year when a carpenter from Germany by the name of Bruno Richard Hauptman would die for the kidnapping and murder of the small son of the flying hero Charles A. Lindbergh.

And a national election would put incumbent Franklin D. Roosevelt and his "New Deal" back at the helm in a campaign that would have as one of its candidates a Communist by the name of Earl Browder . . .

The desert flora, rich from winter rains, that met the traveling couple changed quickly into stark white as they moved across mile-high mountains and flat plains, still frozen under a blanket of ice and snow. Shortly those very plains would echo to the bawl of hungry cattle who would be mocked in their hunger by the dry burnt earth.

But the pioneer and his wife were concerned about another hunger — the spiritual hunger of needy children. This is what drove them from city to city. They stopped only long enough to ignite a fire in understanding hearts — and then went on.

In that "impossible" trip, J. Irvin Overholtzer saw his dream for reaching children crystallize in flesh-and-blood people forming themselves into responsible committees in almost every major city in the nation and Canada. State and city directors were appointed and a program of children's home Bible classes, soon to be known as Good News Clubs, was set up.

From border to border — the Pacific to the Atlantic, North to South — people were touched by his tears and brought to see their responsibility to win the children of their area to Christ.

He enlisted full-time workers — such as the Rev. Walter Werner, preacher in Topeka, who at the response of his burdened voice on the telephone met him and accepted appointment as CEF head for Kansas; Blanche Gallagher of Salt Lake City, local Bible teacher of note who became a state director and later a teacher in the Child Evangelism Institute; Shirley Wisner, a convert of Dr. Walter L. Wilson and teacher in his Kansas City Bible school who, lighted by the quick touch of his torch, set out on a soul-winning ministry to children that never stopped; Gwendolin C. Armour, in whose office the first committee meeting of the nation had met. As Chicago's director she later saw six hundred classes for children held in her city and personally won many children on the street to Christ.

The privations were there. They always would be, he knew. One day, in Omaha, with that mercilessly cold winter still hanging on in the plain state of Nebraska, the native-born Californian had to pawn his overcoat to get money. A new overcoat to replace it was several cities away.

Only one thing mattered: obedience to God and the vision.

Believers in city after city caught his burden for the children: Denver, Des Moines, Kansas City . . .

While in Indianapolis he made a decision. He would visit the South! Someone had earlier told him, "Child Evangelism Fellowship cannot be organized in the South. Denominationalism is too strong." This remark simply challenged Mr. Overholtzer to more prayer. The burden for the children of the South became heavy upon his heart.

From Indianapolis, he made a "side" trip to Nashville, to Birmingham, and then Atlanta.

"In the Tabernacle Baptist Church of Atlanta I was greatly blessed by the preaching of Dr. W. H. Knight, a prominent Southern Baptist. He gave me an interview and took much time to get full information about the child evangelism movement. At the close I pressed him: 'We need some leaders to sponsor CEF in the South. I believe if you would become a member of the National Committee the whole South would open up to this movement. You need not consider the matter now, but promise me you'll make it a matter of prayer.'

"'That,' said Dr. Knight, 'will take a lot of praying!'"

Months later a letter from the kindly Southern pastor indicated that he was ready to serve. Exuberant, Mr. Overholtzer wrote him, "Heaven alone will record what your decision will mean to the hosts of children — Negro and white — in the many Southern states!"

Every Southern state since has had an active ministry among children.

Philadelphia was then the third largest metropolis in the U.S. The cradle of the nation was pegged as a key to open up the Eastern seaboard.

Overholtzer arrived there after a stop in Pittsburgh where Dr. Harold J. Ockenga, then pastor of Point Breeze Presbyterian Church, gladly lent his name as a supporter of the work.

In Philadelphia "the evangelical Christian leaders backed us one hundred percent," Mr. O said. "The Philadelphia School of the Bible and the Bible Institute of Pennsylvania [now merged to Philadelphia College of Bible] invited me to address their students."

His host in Philadelphia, Dr. E. Schuyler English, introduced him to Dr. Charles G. Trumbull, editor of *The Sunday School Times*. How pleased he was to meet this Christian leader whose writings on the victorious Christian life had been a beacon in his struggles to find scriptural truth on the subject. The influential periodical became an early promoter of the cause of child evangelism and helped greatly to advance the work.

Wilmington . . . Washington, D. C. . . . Baltimore . . .

Dr. T. Roland Philips, pastor of the great Arlington Presbyterian Church, became chairman of the CEF committee for Baltimore and a member of the Child Evangelism Fellowship Advisory Council. He remained a true friend of the work.

And then there was the nation's largest city. Overholtzer literally dreaded to go to New York City.

"From the moment of my call, Satan had kept New York City before me as the place where I would fail. I did not know a soul in the great city of skyscrapers."

When it came time to leave the friendly contacts of the City of Brotherly Love to go north, he was without funds!

God provided in a gift from the Rev. Herbert Hoag, assistant pastor of Berachah Church, a congregation with a warm interest in the evangelization of children. Without knowing his need, Hoag pressed fifty dollars into his hand. This became an unforgettable experience to the evangelist, who walked with one hand outstretched in behalf of the children and the other up to God for His supply.

Someone told Overholtzer to contact a certain Clarence E. Mason when he got to New York. Mason gave him the names of spiritual leaders.

"Many palatial offices were visited where I found real men of God in high positions in the business world."

When the president of the Nickel Bank sent word that he did not have time to see his visitor, Mr. O sent word back, "I will just wait until you can see me." The man did.

The noted lawyer James E. Bennet was one of a number who joined in support of Child Evangelism. In fact, an organizational meeting was set up in his office.

Spiritually frigid New England had its warm churches

and warm souls like Dr. C. Gordon Brownville of Tremont Temple and Dr. J. Elwin Wright of the New England Fellowship. Both men backed the movement.

Like a force you cannot stop Overholtzer moved, seemingly by an unseen hand, into French Canada, to Toronto, back to the Midwest and across into Western Canada.

In every place friends were brought into the work. Unit after unit was organized for the movement. In some places, people already concerned about the mounting need among the children had been waiting for something like Child Evangelism Fellowship to happen.

Key targets for the man with an eye for organization and expansion, both in this historic trip in 1936 and later, were Christian schools of higher learning. "Get the leaders," was his philosophy, "and you'll get the people."

He got them — men such as Dr. V. Raymond Edman, president of Wheaton College; Dr. John F. Walvoord, of Dallas Theological Seminary; Dr. Judson A. Rudd, president of William Jennings Bryan University; the Rev. L. E. Maxwell, founder and president of Prairie Bible Institute — and many others.

These men lent their names to the movement, their influence to its support. Their students listened to the challenge of Overholtzer as in the chapels he preached to them his one sermon: Matthew 18:1-14. He emphasized verse 14, his heartbeat: "Even so it is not the will of your Father which is in heaven, that one of these little ones should perish."

Dr. Henry C. Thiessen of the Wheaton College faculty became a lifelong friend and counselor, giving keen advice in the setting up of organizational details such as the constitution and bylaws.

One man Overholtzer had his heart set on was not easy to convince: Dr. Rowland V. Bingham, founder and head of the Sudan Interior Mission. Mr. O believed he needed him to open Toronto. At first Bingham would not see him. Finally he consented.

"As I talked," said Mr. O, "he answered again and again, 'There must be no more Christian organizations in Toronto.'" Overholtzer was sympathetic. He too had felt there were too many organizations when God called him to organize Child Evangelism Fellowship. But God had ordered.

"Dear man of God that he was," said Overholtzer, "the Lord seemed to speak to him." At last Bingham gave his approval. "I trust he knows what his decision has meant to the children of Canada."

It had always troubled the founder of CEF that he had wasted so much of his life. First, he had wandered for years in sin. Then, for sixteen years he had preached salvation by works. Another sixteen years, victory by works. One day, in desperation, he had sought God for encouragement. The Lord gave him the assurance of Joel 2:25 — "I will restore to you the years that the locust hath eaten. . . ."

God was restoring!

Overholtzer's travels continued back and forth across the country. After he had visited the large cities, he turned to the next in size.

It was sometimes difficult for Anna to travel with him. At such times she remained with some of their children in California. They all were now married and had homes of their own.

One day, alone, in Wichita, Kansas, in April, 1938, word came: *Mother's had a heart attack.* Although he left at once for California, it was impossible to reach her before she had slipped away.

Jesse would always be grateful for her faithfulness and loyalty in the days of beginnings. He thought of that large, long, cross-country trip they had taken together in that historic year of openings and beginnings. Of the financial privations. Of the times unending of waiting upon God for the next move and the next mouthful. Now the work in many of these same cities was beginning to mushroom. Hundreds upon hundreds of children were coming to know Jesus Christ as Saviour and growing spiritually as they gathered in the weekly Good News Clubs.

How glad I am Anna lived to see some of the fruit of our labors, he thought as he remembered their years together.

I think the idea of going to the mission field is crazy, but here is a one-hundred-dollar check to help finance it.

16

South to the Harvest

The blue 1937 Ford braked to a halt beside the uniformed *oficial de aduana* at the Mexican customs in Nuevo Laredo.

"May I see your card, *Señor?*"

The man at the wheel thrust his hand into his coat pocket and produced a three-dollar tourist pass. The official stamped it "March 22, 1939."

The sixty-two-year-old motorist took the card, studied it for a moment, then smiled. He pulled the gear shift into low, released the clutch and began to move into the strange new land. At that moment "International" Child Evangelism Fellowship became an actual fact although the organization had been incorporated as such two years before on May 20, 1937.[1]

---

[1] In April, 1966, International and National Child Evangelism Fellowship Committees and their ministries were officially merged to "Child Evangelism Fellowship Incorporated." There is now only one governing board.

Mr. O drove slowly at first through the noisy streets of Nuevo Laredo, soaking up the "feel" of a foreign land. It was like traveling backward in time. Suddenly the open road of the Pan American Highway stretched before him. The engine began to pick up speed and his heart sang with it.

Past the overloaded buses, bulging with passengers and poultry, he drove; through the wide stretches of desert with their fiery-red cactus blooms. All the while, he prayed for the children.

The trip was a puzzle to many of Mr. O's friends. Europe was at war. The U.S. was still languishing in economic depression. And Child Evangelism Fellowship was in its early developmental stages.

"I think the idea of going to the mission field is crazy," one man wrote. Then he succumbed to the judgment of his friend and added, "but here's a one-hundred-dollar check to help finance it."

Mr. O viewed his work with impatience. Already nearing the traditional age for retirement, he attempted to do the work of a lifetime in his sunset years. Heavily underscored in his Bible is Isaiah 50:7, "I set my face like a flint, and I know that I shall not be ashamed."

Mexico was the first step on the journey. "How thrilling it is," he exclaimed in a letter home, "to drive on the fine Pan American Highway with one consuming passion — that the children of Mexico might be evangelized!" The highway which took him to the capital city had been completed only nine months earlier — the first section of the system which eventually would link Alaska with Argentina.

Toward evening of the second day a quick check of his road map made his heart leap. He was approaching the village of Valles for his first prearranged speaking engagement in a foreign land. Soon he was bumping along into the driveway of the Huasteca Mission.

Here for the first time his message was interpreted. To

gaze into the sea of brown faces was to have his call confirmed. Missionary Janie Love became the first adult fruit of his southern crusade. Following her agreement to serve as the Child Evangelism Fellowship representative for that area, he sped on to other towns and villages.

In Tomazunchale he was guest of Dr. J. G. Dale, founder of the Mexican Indian Mission. This man who had built a Bible training school for the Aztec Indians became interested in Mr. O's crusade and served as a member of the Child Evangelism Advisory Council.

Another link was forged in the lengthening chain of responsible leaders.

In Mexico City Overholtzer was guest of the Rev. N. W. Taylor, director of all Presbyterian missions in Latin America. Taylor gave Mr. O his full attention. He arranged speaking engagements in flourishing churches such as the great Presbyterian Church of Mexico City. The pastor, the noted Rev. Eliezar Perez, became an enthusiast for Child Evangelism. The visit of Mr. O to the mile-and-a-half-high city was the start of an extensive outreach to children there. The very first training class for CEF in Mexico was held in Perez's church.

In Mexico City the pioneer found a place to park his car and bought his first plane ticket. He flew to Guatemala, El Salvador, Honduras, Nicaragua and Costa Rica and made various side trips. In Guatemala City the Rev. Frank Toms, pioneer missionary of the Central American Mission, gave Mr. O helpful advice in missionary strategy.

"The counsel given here," Mr. O wrote, "shaped our decisions for further development and gave the work success in other fields."

There were visits to Bible institutes, conferences with missionaries, meetings with boys and girls who sat enthralled as Mr. O turned the pages of his little Wordless Book.

The traveler was smitten by his hosts, the missionaries. "I am not able to express my high esteem of their nobility," he said. "Each seems to be in just the right place. I found that every child of five years or older in the missionaries' families had already received Christ as his Saviour."

The Baptists, Presbyterians, the Central American Mission, Latin America Mission, Friends Mission and Evangelical Mission all heartily welcomed him. He in turn challenged them to expect real results among Spanish-speaking boys and girls.

Deep impressions were made on those he met. A CEF missions executive visiting this area thirty years later said, "People still talk about him and his visit. They remember him as a person. And they remember his mission and his burden."

Scenes he remembered longest were those in which he directly touched the lives of the children. In Guatemala City a hundred youngsters responded to his appeal for salvation following a service in a Central American Mission church. In San Salvador the mission invited him to speak at a rally where fifty children received the Saviour.

A couple of missionaries' children were overheard to say, "Do you know Mr. Overholtzer? *He loves children!*"

"Well I should say I do know that! He ate dinner at our house!"

His whirlwind blitz of Central America at an end, Mr. O flew back to Mexico City. He made his way to the border by car and arrived in San Antonio, Texas, on the first day of May, after six weeks out of the country.

In San Antonio another significant event occurred which was worthy of a flag on the chart of his personal agenda. On May 4, 1939, he was married to Ruth Pennebaker. A graduate of the Bible Institute of Los Angeles (now Biola College), she had served with the Presbyterian mission board in Alaska and among Spanish-speaking people in Los Angeles before joining Child Evangelism Fellowship.

The combined talents of J. Irvin and Ruth Overholtzer were spent together in a work that strengthened the home base of operations and lit the fires of concern for children in every continent during the sixteen years God gave them to share.

San Antonio . . . a little "doll house," as their friends came to call it . . . a postage-stamp yard in which Overholtzer planted five Mahan paper-shell pecan trees, Texas bluebonnets and California poppies . . .

For five years a small study in the Overholtzer home in the colorful City of the Alamo, Gateway to the South, served as personal headquarters for the fledgling organization. The crusader settled here for several reasons. He wanted to open this area for CEF. It was near Dallas, the home of several mission boards and the well-respected Dallas Theological Seminary. And it was close to the Latin American mission fields.

Correspondence began building up. "How do we do this? How do we do that?" Seemingly a thousand things had to be discussed, prayed over and dispensed with in the beginning and developing of the work. Mr. O, to the point, in short shrift handled the problems. One letter in his files contained a mere eighteen words!

"Why did he have to be so short?" some complained. But the crusader had no time nor inclination for frills and fussing. The work must go on!

In the summer of 1939, despite the threat of a global war, Mr. O, constrained by the Holy Spirit, began his plans to spread the child evangelism fires to South America.

The air was filled with suspicion — Russia and Japan were at odds with each other over the Manchukuo situation . . . Mussolini, dictator of Italy, had moved in to conquer helpless Ethiopia . . . and Hitler and his army had knocked off country after country in Europe in his thirst to conquer the world. On September 1 he marched his army into Poland.

With screaming newspaper headlines, Overholtzer quietly

plotted his tour: his plans — to visit every country in South America and lay the groundwork for reaching the children.

He assiduously corresponded with missionaries of every evangelical board. Maps and airline schedules were everywhere. Information was massed on each country. He ate and slept Latin America.

"Do you think we should go?" Mrs. Overholtzer asked, following Great Britain and France's declaration of war on Germany on September 3.

"Why not?" asked the indomitable crusader.

Mr. O had to undergo three major surgical operations before they could go. As in the breaking the Lord had put him through in Chicago before the launching of the work in the United States, so it seemed the Lord was breaking him before the extensive launch abroad.

"He would never get down," says Ruth Overholtzer. "He was the perennial optimist — always cheerful. When things got really rough, he would say in the words of the song of those war days, 'Praise the Lord and pass the ammunition!' "

On Christmas Day Mr. and Mrs. Overholtzer climbed aboard a train, bound for Miami, where they would enplane. Mr. O's feet were so sore from recent foot surgery, he could hardly stand the pressure of shoes. As he stepped across the depot platform, his wife asked him, "Do you think we're ready?"

"Ready for what?" asked Mr. O.

"Why, ready to challenge the South American continent with the spiritual needs of the children!"

Mr. O chuckled and replied, "More unlikely instruments could not be found, but God has promised to use the weak things."

Pan American's "phenomenon of the skies" in those pre-jet days would wing the Overholtzers 13,000 miles on their mission for the children, around the whole of South America and into parts of the West Indies. This three-month tour included visits to twenty-one countries. With the power of

2800 horses, the silver chariot would take them across steaming jungles, over desolate arid valleys, through breathtaking mountain grandeur, past lush banana and coffee plantations.

Cities like Havana, Kingston, Lima and São Paulo would be more than just names. They would be palm-lined streets . . . women carrying heavy loads of fruit and vegetables and pottery on their heads . . . old Inca ruins . . . and, most significant of all, they would mean children, lots of children, who needed to be reached for the Lord Jesus.

Practically every evangelical mission board was contacted. Most responded, with volunteer representatives being appointed in every place. Key men were added to the growing council of reference, the Advisory Council.

"Isn't it just wonderful," Mr. O would say to his hosts as he alighted from the plane, "what God is doing to win the children these days!" Enthusiastically he told of God at work in the United States, Canada, in Mexico and Central America.

His ardor quickly struck fire with the missionaries as this new emphasis on winning children was introduced. Plans were made for beginning Good News Clubs among the children and translating teaching materials into Spanish. In an earlier prayer letter Mr. O had pled with the people of North America to pray for the children of Latin America. God was answering.

A meeting with the Friends Mission in La Paz, Bolivia, lived long in the memory of the touring pair. Mr. O told it repeatedly as he lived again the pioneering days of international outreach.

"The church in the Indian section of the city was crowded, and most of the adults, so colorful in their native dress, were believers. The women, in bright shawls and skirts, removed their babies from their backs to the floor during the meeting. How they listened as their pastor interpreted into the Indian tongue my message on the Wordless

Book! How their faces would light up with understanding — the children's too! Then at the close the pastor gave an altar call for the children to accept Christ. How wonderful it was to see them come one by one until about thirty-five were gathered at the altar. The pastor dealt with each personally and faithfully, and I am sure many were born again that day. This meeting alone, in all of its marvelous aspects, was worth the trip to South America."

Island-hopping, with stops in Trinidad, Puerto Rico, Dominican Republic and Haiti, completed the Overholtzers' first large overseas tour for the *cause celebre*. The trip begun in pain had ended in a pageant of triumph.

The "frosting on the cake" was hearing from the lips of the Rev. and Mrs. Harry Briault, British missionaries who were their hosts in Recife, Brazil, that they felt God leading them to be directors for the vast area of Brazil. They became the first full-time CEF workers overseas.

A few years later, on December 4, 1944, following their graduation from Moody Bible Institute, the Rev. and Mrs. Arthur Phillips, who had worked in the Chicago CEF office, left for Mexico to become directors for that needy land. The second couple to enter full-time work for the Fellowship outside of the United States had also gone South to the Harvest.

One good thing World War II is doing is to cause us to study the map of the world. May the Spirit of God convict us of the small portion of it to which we have taken the Gospel.

17

To the Children of the World

One passion drove J. Irvin Overholtzer to make plans to enter other foreign lands: the spiritual neglect of the world's children.

His call was worldwide.

With his visits to Latin America well received, he longed to share the concern of his heart with Christian workers around the world.

To him, "Jesus loves the little children, red and yellow, black and white" was not just a little Sunday school song. It was a Holy-Spirit impressed reality. Prostrate before God he had received his commission.

Limitations of health and strength and world conditions caused J. Irvin Overholtzer's foreign travels to cease with his South American trip. How his heart ached for the children of the rest of the world — children of India, Japan, the South Seas — children he would never see except through the eyes of another.

"Jesus gave a global commission," he wrote, "but we are so provincial, so self-centered, so sinful that we use our time, our talents, our money in such a way that we are blind and callous regarding the precious children who literally sit in darkness." He added significantly, "One good thing World War II is doing is to cause us to study the map of the world. May the Spirit of God convict us of the small portion of it to which we have taken the Gospel."

Increasing administrative responsibilities kept him more and more at home base.

But Jesse Overholtzer *did* touch every major country, and many minor ones, through the ministries God enabled him to found: a monthly magazine — an outgrowth of which was a large literature program of full-color visualized children's Bible lessons — and a school for training CEF leaders.

While bombs from Japanese planes were screaming into Pearl Harbor at the start of the United States' participation in World War II, a little knot of Dallas Seminary students huddled over a table putting the finishing touches on an exciting editorial project, *Child Evangelism* magazine.

Through the pages of this monthly magazine the evangelical world was informed of what God was doing in the winning of children. In practical how-to-do-it sections, edited by Ruth Overholtzer, teachers remote from training classes were taught techniques to attract children and help them to understand how to be saved and grow in the Christian life. Through the magazine, the work was unified and solidified, and in its columns Mr. O had the opportunity to bring his challenge around the globe in what became his pulpit of paper and ink.

The CEF founder had had his first brush with printer's ink in his home town forty years earlier when he established

The Lordsburg Sunbeam. He had seen the power of print in putting over ideas and multiplying a cause. He believed that "God's message, clothed in paper and ink, empowered by God's Spirit as God's men publish, distribute, and pray for it has God's promise that it will not return unto Him void."

Letter after letter arrived at headquarters warming the heart of the crusader. Laymen were challenged to win children. Pastors were apprised of the merits of such a work. And teachers were introduced to a new method of illustration in the popular flannelgraph lesson first appearing as an insert in the *Child Evangelism* magazine and later produced as separate series.

This monthly magazine feature became the *piece de resistance* in soliciting new subscribers. Child Evangelism Fellowship led the field in visual aid techniques. These became the flying wedge that opened up many new associations, too — especially on the foreign field. Beginning with materials in Spanish for Latin America, the CEF lessons soon found their way into the languages of the people in Brazil, France, Germany, Japan, China, India and finally to nearly every major country.

Teacher training books written by CEF's founder were also translated and distributed around the world.

"The use of visual aids is new," commented Mr. O. "We will make mistakes in using them and we invite criticism of our literature and will gladly make corrections where necessary."

A missionary in Latin America was quick to reply to that offer. She objected to the use of pictures to relate Bible stories. "As Protestants," she wrote, "we should not lend credence to the viewpoint that images are needed in worship."

Replied the pioneer: "Tell the children that these pictures were painted by an artist who *thought* Jesus may have looked this way. They are only a teaching aid and not an end in themselves. Use the visuals to make clear to the children the great Bible doctrines of our Christian faith."

And the visual aids rolled on!

In Australia teachers were found tacking their flannelgraphs to wooden telephone poles in suburban streets and gathering children for the lesson.

In Japan they were propped up on the floor as children in stocking feet sat around on the *tatami* mats.

In the Scandinavian countries they were displayed in quaint homes of rural areas where children in bright clothing gathered to be instructed.

A missionary in Peiping, China, said she didn't have enough money left over to subscribe for the magazine but was preparing to cut down on food in order to keep the periodical coming to her station. She wore out her flannelgraph board lugging it over the rough trails and had to have one built for each station so she could leave it behind.

A missionary subscriber in India was elated by his first issue. "Yesterday I gave the first lesson on *The Bible, the Word of God* in one of our Christian meetings," he said. "It was well received. Everyone was spellbound and so reverent."

One staff member called the magazine the "John the Baptist" for Child Evangelism Fellowship. It went ahead of the workers to prepare the way for the introduction of the movement.

Victor E. Cory, president of Scripture Press and longtime friend of the Overholtzers, wrote: "I wonder if many people write you of the inspiration and uplift from reading the columns of *Child Evangelism* magazine. I feel I must pass on my feeling of gratitude to Him and to you. Of course you don't have to dream up the contents. You just have to chronicle the thrilling events as they happen."

The nation's choice manpower was at battle on two foreign fronts. Industry was desperately in need of employees to win World War II and many couples worked long shifts in war plants across the nation.

Gasoline and tires were rationed, travel was restricted to barest essentials and public transportation was crowded beyond capacity.

But the man in a hurry couldn't wait for a war to close to begin another vital project. Calls began coming in for directors and missionaries to develop the child evangelism program in areas he had visited at home and overseas.

At the height of the war, on January 2, 1945, also in the city of Dallas, Mr. Overholtzer and several co-workers began the Child Evangelism Institute. It was planned as a short, concentrated orientation and guidance course in which Bible college and institute graduates could be trained for the specialized field of children's work.

Studies included Bible doctrine, lesson and teacher preparation, administration and business. Heavy emphasis was laid on the importance, challenge and methods of evangelizing children and helping them in Christian development. The course was six months, later reduced to three.

The charter student body numbered thirty. They came from fifteen states, two Canadian provinces and the Republic of Ecuador. They represented ten colleges and twelve Bible institutes and came from fourteen different denominations.

For the one who had seen his Chicago dream for a school crumble like a bombed building, the founding of a school for training CEF leadership worldwide was almost more than he could take. Mrs. Overholtzer recalls her husband being so overcome with tears of joy he could not finish his first message to the students.

Essentially a teacher rather than a preacher, Overholtzer was thrilled to be back in the teaching ministry again. Face to face with those who would carry the torch to such countries as Africa, India, Quebec, Europe and Latin America, he shared the trials and triumphs of the unfolding child evangelism vision.

"You're going to see this school big some day," he told the students. "Other schools will be patterned after it around the world."

His prediction came true as one after another graduate of this the mother school went beyond the United States to set up such schools in Japan, Brazil, the Philippines and Mexico. Today they are being held in twelve countries. The parent school now holds three sessions annually.[1]

Graduation exercises for this first session of the school that would graduate hundreds of child evangelism specialists were held on Flag Day, 1945, in the Scofield Memorial Church. Dr. John Walvoord, then registrar and professor of theology at Dallas Theological Seminary, spoke on the topic "Why Preach to Children?"

Fourteen of the graduates scattered to foreign shores to open or develop the work of child evangelism. Others became local and state leaders.

Overholtzer's vision found its fruition in leaders, volunteers, and faithful financial and prayer supporters. Most will be unnamed. Even the ones named prefer that they not be. But without them, the picture is incomplete.

Mrs. Joseph F. Cannon and her daughter of North Carolina and Mrs. Leo Brown of Chicago, to mention only a few, were of the very first who gave faithfully that these who

---

[1] In the middle 1940's the administrative office, the Chicago literature depot, Child Evangelism Institute and *Child Evangelism* magazine were consolidated and brought to the Los Angeles area. They remained here until 1959. At this time under the guidance of H. J. Taylor, noted Chicago industrialist who had succeeded Dr. Paul W. Rood as chairman of the International Child Evangelism Fellowship Committee, the headquarters was moved to Grand Rapids, Mich. CEF Institute was located on its own property at Wolf Lake, near Muskegon.

had volunteered their lives for the children overseas might be able to get there with the message so much needed.

The Jack Pine is a curious little tree. Its seed can lie on the side of a mountain for years without sprouting. Then suddenly a forest fire sweeps across the face of the slope. The intense heat cracks open the hard cone and a tiny shoot soon appears above the burnt ground. As the years pass, its roots go deeper and deeper as the Jack Pine reaches farther and farther toward the sky.

The Jack Pine owes its birth to adversity.

In some ways, Child Evangelism Fellowship is like the Jack Pine seedling. Born in the Depression, it was organized by the hit-run tactics of a little-known promoter. It struggled to its feet during the worst war in the history of the world.

All these served but to sear the "Jack Pine" seedlings of the baby organization and to cause them to root deeper and grow taller in the wilderness of spiritual child neglect.

"You have to *have* a dream to see one fulfilled," Jesse Overholtzer used to say.

God privileged him to see his.

A tally in March, 1955, a few months before he passed away, showed Child Evangelism Fellowship operating in sixty countries.

More than one hundred fifty overseas workers were on the field or under appointment.

Full-time workers at home and in Canada directing the local and state operation numbered in the hundreds.

Nothing can stop the force of an idea whose time has come.

History was ripe for Child Evangelism.

We have only a little while to win those warmhearted, friendly little immortal souls who are everywhere and are everywhere the same.

— Gwendolin C. Armour

18

The Same in Any Language

Like little jewels they began to shine around the world — children won to Christ through the ministry of Child Evangelism Fellowship workers.

Whether of one country or another, their response was the same. The boys and girls thrilled to hear about a loving Saviour who could forgive their sins and come into their hearts to live.

Having received Christ, their lives became potent witness of His transforming power.

Johnny[1] was only seven, but in his home town in Sweden he was known as the worst rowdy. He was constantly in trouble. Frequent whippings by his mother seemed of no

---

[1] Fictitious names have been used for the children.

avail. He went to Sunday school but only because he was forced to.

"Say, Johnny," someone called to him one day, "there's going to be a Bible club in our neighborhood. Would you like to come?"

To Johnny *Bible* meant only one thing.

"Church? In the middle of the week?"

Curiosity drove him to find out what it was all about. He was in for a surprise. "Good News Club" was fun. Real fun! His playmates were there. They sang happy songs. And the pleasant-looking teacher made the Bible story come alive with pictures that stuck like magic to a flannelboard!

One thing the teacher said really surprised him. She said that all the children were sinners! *Me, a sinner?* thought Johnny. *I always go to Sunday school!*

But the statement was convincing, coming right from the Bible. Johnny had been brought up to have great respect for God's Book.

"There is a way to get rid of your sin," continued the teacher. "You need to receive Jesus Christ into your heart and He will cleanse your heart from sin. Jesus died for you on the Cross. He took your punishment because He loves you very much."

Loves me? mused Johnny. *I didn't think anybody did.*

The truth gripped him deeply. Then and there he decided to ask this Jesus to come into his heart.

Johnny became a different boy. Instead of a troublemaker he became a blessing. He even asked permission of his public school teacher to tell his classmates the story that had changed his life. And she granted it.

Today, a grown man, Johnny is serving the Lord in his home country following study at a Bible school in the United States.

In her stumbling French the young American missionary was doing her best to try to convey the Gospel message to her Good News Club. She was not prepared for Pierre's sudden outburst: "Jesus *did not* rise from the dead! Jesus *did not* rise from the dead!"

Pierre's father was a Communist. It was obvious that he had trained his son well. And it was certain that Pierre's coming to the club was not to learn what the teacher had to share. But he came, week after week; week after week. He especially delighted in trying to upset the Bible lesson.

Will the Holy Spirit withstand his blatant remarks so that the other children will believe the Bible and not him? the teacher asked herself. She prayed for continued patience.

It happened during the lesson. The teacher had just told the children: "Jesus Christ, the Son of God, can give you a clean heart."

Suddenly Pierre jumped to his feet. The missionary braced herself, expecting the worst.

To her utter amazement, the miniscule anti-God militarist called out anxiously, "What I want to know is how can I have a clean heart?"

With the opening of the spiritual dike, confession flowed freely. "I want to be good," he admitted, "but I can't! I want to tell the truth, but I keep telling lies!"

Then and there the missionary led the young God-defying son of the French Communist to a saving knowledge of Jesus Christ.

Pierre drank in Bible truths as a kitten laps up milk. And the verse that had showed him how he could have a clean heart — "The blood of Jesus Christ, his son, cleanseth us from all sin" — became his favorite.

Patsy, a little four year old who lived in the United States, never missed Good News Club. In that club she too received Jesus Christ as her Saviour.

Promptly, on returning home from the club, Patsy shared the Bible lesson with her parents. This she continued to do, week after week.

One day on coming home from the Good News Club she was unusually busy, rushing hither and thither. Shortly she called, "Time for our class, Mommy! Time for our class, Daddy!"

Her parents took their customary seats.

Then they saw the reason for her busyness. There were to be props for the lesson! On a little table she had set up a checkerboard. In her hand she held two checkers — a black one and a red one. Holding up the black checker little Patsy said to her curious parents, "This stands for sin." Before they had much chance to wonder as to the relevancy of the lesson for them, she said, "People's hearts are dark with sin."[1]

There was no chance for audience rebuttal. Holding up the red checker, she went on: "This stands for the blood of Jesus that takes away sin."

Noticing she didn't have quite enough material to finish illustrating her lesson, Patsy dashed to the bathroom and bounded back, carrying a small piece of white tissue. Holding it up she said, "If you ask Jesus, He will make your heart clean and take away all your sins."

Patsy's mother and father did, not long after this ingenious presentation by their four-year-old daughter-teacher.

On the last day of Child Evangelism camp in Argentina the leader asked for testimonies from the group as to what camp had meant to them. Several responded.

---

[1] Worth noting is Mr. Overholtzer's dislike of the expressions "black heart" and "white heart." He cautioned his workers to impress several things upon the minds of the children relative to the use of the Wordless Book. The word *heart* in Scripture does not refer to the physical heart that pumps blood. It refers to the inner self that thinks and loves and wills; in other words, the "real you." Use of the black page to depict sin and the white page to depict cleansing is merely symbolical. Either red or black could be used to depict sin. The Scriptures use both. But since red is the only color to use to represent blood, black was chosen to represent sin.

"And you, José," asked the leader, "what has camp meant to you? What are you taking home with you that has been a blessing?"

"Nothing! Absolutely nothing! I can't wait to get out of here!" José blurted out. Though he had been the object of many prayers on the part of both Christian campers and staff members, he had not yielded to the claims of Christ.

On the bus back to the city, while the other campers laughed and sang and enjoyed themselves, José looked glum. The bus had barely come to a stop at the terminal when he dashed to buy cigarettes.

Here I am, he thought to himself, *back at my old life again.* Lighting a cigarette, he began to smoke.

My old life. Back to my old life. His own thoughts struck him. *What is my old life?*

The answer unreeled before him like a dirty film. He saw the street fights, the gang troubles, the stealing. He thought of some of his friends who were now behind the walls of a correctional institution.

Was this the life he was so eagerly running back to?

The thought gripped him with such force, he threw down his cigarette and ground it with his heel.

"Lord," he prayed in his heart, "I don't want to go back to my old life. Please save me."

Boarding a suburban train for home, José spotted some of his fellow campers.

"José," they cried, "you're singing!"

"I have something to sing about now," he answered. "I'm saved."

José became a strong Christian. Now, as an adult, he is a member of the governing committee of the same camp he was so eager to get away from!

It was happening all over. Children far and wide were hearing the Gospel of Christ, receiving Him as Saviour and sharing the good news with others. Theirs was an uninhibited testimony, a free-flowing witness. Their concern for the spiritual welfare of others was genuine, as seen in little Spanish-speaking Magda in Venezuela.

One day she and several of her playmates who attended the neighborhood Good News Club were having their own little class in her backyard under the mango tree. Magda was the teacher.

"Nobody that's a sinner can go to Heaven unless they believe in the Lord Jesus!" Magda called out. As she did so, she stopped short.

"My daddy's lost! My daddy's lost!" she cried out, her voice breaking. She had suddenly realized the fate of her Gospel-hating father.

Her mother, a Christian, had overheard from the kitchen.

"Ask your friends in Sunday school next Sunday to pray for him," she called out.

"That might be too late!"

Then and there Magda and her little friends, won to Christ in the Good News Club, got down on their knees and prayed for her father. About a year later he too received Christ and united his home in Christian faith and worship.

Three young Portuguese boys listened especially well as the teacher of the Good News Club told about Jesus. She said that He loved them — yes, all the boys and girls and men and women of Portugal and of the whole world! She told them about Jesus dying for their sins; that He rose again from the dead; that He would take away the sins of those who came to Him believingly; that He would make them the very children of God and walk with them day by day.

Those three young boys were among the first to respond in that first Good News Club in Portugal. Today, grown men, all three are in full-time Christian service. Two are pastors in Portugal. The third is a missionary in Mozambique, off the east coast of Africa.

Mike was just an ordinary "cute" kid living in a Western United States city. But he was not what you would call a happy boy, probably because of problems at home. Often his father was away. And his mother was burdened trying to keep their little family together.

One day someone invited Mike to the neighborhood Good News Club. A young high school girl was the teacher.

Mike was impressed. *She acts like she's got something*, he thought as he listened to the vivacious young lady. She would dramatize the Bible stories — dramatize them in such a way that Mike could practically see David slay that giant Goliath. And when she told about Jesus feeding five thousand men with the little boy's lunch, he felt like he was *right there* on the Galilean hillside.

What Mike thought was the greatest was hearing from his teacher that Jesus loved him — so much so that He had given His life for him.

Mike knew he was a sinner even before the teacher quoted the Bible verse from Romans 3: "All have sinned and come short of the glory of God." But the teacher said that because Christ had died, had taken his punishment, he wouldn't be punished for his sin if he took Him for his very own Saviour.

By the sofa in the den in that little white frame house near his home Mike knelt with his teen-aged teacher and asked Jesus to be his Saviour.

Little did Mike realize that God had great plans for him. Today, a pastor, he is serving one of the fastest growing churches of his denomination. Not forgetting the importance of ministering to children, each Sunday morning, before his sermon, he brings an evangelistic object lesson to the children. He trains and supervises evangelistic teams of men and women who go out every week into the neighborhood to help men and women and boys and girls to receive Christ just as he did in the Good News Club.

"Butch is a real problem," a friend told the Good News Club teacher in Southern California. "He goes from foster home to foster home. Nobody can keep him. He's terribly resentful about his home breaking up and his parents getting a divorce. He's just impossible!"

But the Good News Club teacher knew that with God there is no such thing as an "impossible" child.

In the club Butch was like a Mexican jumping bean. He just couldn't be still. He was not mean, but he was constantly restless, shoving around and annoying the other children.

This isn't going to be easy, the teacher thought to herself.

Finally it was Bible time. The lesson was on Heaven.

"A wonderful place," the teacher said as she described the unbelievable beauties of God's dwelling place. "The street is made of pure gold. There is a river clear as crystal. And there is a tree that gives twelve different kinds of fruit!"

With each new startling thing he heard, Butch's eyes grew bigger and bigger.

"And there nobody ever gets sick. Nobody ever gets angry. Nobody ever is sad. Everybody is happy *all the time.* For this is God's House, and there is no sin there to spoil it."

Butch became very quiet. *Could it be — Could it be —*

He raised his hand to venture the all-important question: "Are there any foster homes in Heaven?"

"No, Butch, there are no foster homes in Heaven."

With one bound, Butch was on his feet. "Hey, kids! Hey, kids!" he shouted, waving his hands in unrestrained excitement. "*No foster homes in Heaven! No foster homes in Heaven!*" With that he sat down and quietly listened to the rest of the Bible lesson. When the teacher gave the invitation, hand-me-down Butch received Christ with alacrity and rejoiced to know he was bound for this wonderful place that Christ had gone to prepare even for him.

Such true-life stories are the weekly norm in the ministry of Child Evangelism Fellowship in its outreach to children around the world. Their cries, their laughter and their love are after all the same in any language.

The grace of God is the dynamo of Heaven, working night and day, all the time, to accomplish things for us and in us that we can never accomplish for ourselves.

— Charles G. Trumbull, D.D.

19

Grace All the Way

Hands that have guided a large and growing work from its beginning do not easily yield the reins to another's grasp. Yet when the "keepers of the house" began to tremble and "those that look out of the windows" were darkened, Mr. O passed the torch with bold, firm action to his successor.

The conduct of the pioneer in the transfer of leadership is remembered by those who observed it as the practical outworking of the grace of God in a life totally committed to Him.

Mr. O was assured that Child Evangelism Fellowship was "God's work, not mine." He believed God was abundantly able to carry it forward without him.

On his seventy-fifth birthday, July 20, 1952, year of his

"retirement," members of the headquarters office staff and friends gathered in the Overholtzer home in Pacific Palisades, near Los Angeles, where the Overholtzers had lived since the CEF offices had been brought to the West Coast.

In response to expressions of goodwill Mr. O distilled the years into one characteristically brief statement: "It was all by God's grace alone." God gave him three more years.

He continued to teach a few courses at the Child Evangelism Institute, held in the headquarters building in Pacific Palisades. He watched with misty eyes as CEF missionaries came and went. In the chapel they told of children of many backgrounds and races receiving Christ as Saviour. Those who cast a glance at a certain seat in the fourth row could see an old man reach into his pocket for his handkerchief and slowly wipe his eyes. Or was it too sacred to notice?

His step was slow now, his voice broken. But the feeling of responsibility for winning children remained.

"I'm very burdened that people evangelize the children, *not* because *we* say so, but because *it is commanded in the Word of God*," he told a staff member.

In his younger days of shunting back and forth across the continent people thought of him as the man of the map and the Book. Now, with slower gait and limited strength, he hovered much over his world globe. He would spot a country, check its population in his atlas, make a note of it and pray for someone to go.

One friend said, "Some of the countries Mr. O mentioned for prayer I didn't even know were on the map, let alone that they needed missionaries!"

As Mr. O's eyes grew poorer he sometimes found diversion from his work in television "Westerns." He probably saw in them his own father and mother crossing the plains in wild, lawless country.

He was able to read large print under bright lights. But he agreed that perhaps his eyes were worse than he thought the day he opened the medicine cabinet and mistakenly swallowed a teaspoonful of shoe polish instead of the liquid vitamins he was looking for!

The veteran evangelist constantly followed his workers in prayer. They were, it seemed, a part of his very soul. Not only did he pray for them and their work but he prayed by name for the nationals who worked with them. The missionary who opened Portugal for Child Evangelism told of her visit with Mr. O during furlough. "The Lord had raised up many helpers," she said. "When back in California I discovered that Mr. Overholtzer had memorized the names of these folk and was faithfully remembering them in prayer!"

Mr. O continued to write his column " Prayer with Thanksgiving" in *Child Evangelism* magazine. In it he told about the need for missionaries. He wrote of advances on the fields. And he gave suggestions for prayer. In his last published words he requested prayer for missionaries in Lebanon and in the Hawaiian Islands.

Probably thinking of the worldwide work and what still waited to be accomplished, he wrote: "How wonderful to know that no matter how strong are the forces who possess the land to be conquered, if the thing to be undertaken falls within the scope of God's promises, through prayer it *can be done*. More than that, it *will be done*. We are dealing with the living God. He is able. He keeps His *every* promise. *But His promises must be claimed in prayer.*"

Students who sat in Mr. O's classes would best remember him for the truths that had cost him the most. But probably their greatest lesson was Mr. O himself. "If you don't think God can use you," he would tell them, "look at me. See what God did through a nobody. He'll use you too if you keep fully yielded to Him and trust Him to work through you."

One of Mr. O's favorite quotations — "Faithful is he that calleth you, who also will do it" (I Thess. 5:24) — became his traditional blessing on each graduating class of the institute. He knew whereof he spoke. For it was grace all the way — from his jubilant stepladder experience of assurance of salvation to his handing down the leadership of the organization God had founded through him.

For he shall be as a tree planted by the waters, and that spreadeth out her roots . . . neither shall cease from yielding fruit. — Jeremiah 17:8

20

As a Tree

A springtime breeze lifted the sweet breath of flowers into the air as Mr. O walked on the velvet-green lawn in the garden of his home.

He sniffed the orange blossoms on his "one-tree grove" as he had done many years before on his ranch. His other trees too — persimmon, avocado, fig and walnut — were thriving, he noticed.

Often his heart yearned for a stately Mahan paper-shell pecan tree. He had come to love them down there in his adopted state of Texas. They were difficult to grow even there. But he'd like to try one here in his little "grove." His heart still wanted to accept a challenge!

"Darling, I've *got* to have that Mahan paper-shell pecan tree!" he said to Ruth one day. "I wonder if Brother Joe could ship one out from San Antonio."

"But you know it's almost impossible to get it across the border," his wife answered.

Almost impossible, that is. Like his father who had pushed across the rugged Western frontier, J. Irvin Overholtzer was not one to give up.

Many letters passed between California and Texas. One day the coveted seedling arrived.

"Ruthie! It's here! I've got it! My paper-shell pecan!"

His wrinkled hands trembled as he hurriedly cut the twine and pushed aside the wrappings that had protected the delicate tree on its flight.

Mr. O's mind wandered back to the bluebonnet state. He thought of the little cottage and the happy years there. He thought of friends who had stood by him in those difficult days. He thought of the magazine . . . of the school that had been founded whose graduates were now serving around the world. Some were enduring great hardship in order to get the Gospel to the children.

Tenderly he laid the seedling into the cold, black earth . . .

Except a corn of wheat fall into the ground and die, it abideth alone: but if it die, it bringeth forth much fruit. He that loveth his life shall lose it; and he that hateth his life in this world shall keep it unto life eternal (John 12:24, 25).

When J. Irvin Overholtzer quickly and quietly slipped Home to be with the Lord on August 6, 1955, two days after a crippling heart attack, the Mahan paper-shell pecan tree showed no signs of life. Not even the warm California sun filtering through the fresh sea breezes stirred the struggling seedling.

Ruth had suggested earlier, "Let's take it out." After all, it did occupy the center spot on the front lawn of their home on lovely Via de la Paz, "Way of Peace," in the quiet little coast town.

But the farmer grown old, who as a boy looking for fruit had uprooted the first seeds he planted the day after the planting, quietly answered, "Let's dig about it and dung it another year."

Some years later a missionary with Child Evangelism Fellowship home on furlough brought his family to the Overholtzer home for a visit. They chatted with Mrs. O about the far-flung CEF ministries. Then their hostess shared a penciled note that had been safely tucked away in her husband's worn Bible.

"This is Mr. Overholtzer's last prayer memo," she said, her voice stirred with emotion. "He wrote it shortly before he died." On it were such names as New Guinea, New Caledonia, Fiji, the Hebrides and the Solomon Islands with the population of each island noted.

The missionary was at a crossroads in his career. Suddenly something leaped in his heart. He would sow his life in the South Pacific Islands! He would work among the brown-skinned island people, the last for whom Mr. O had prayed! This was the missionary's long-prayed-for answer!

Today to the island of Fiji brown-skinned natives come in outrigger canoes to learn how to lead children to Christ and instruct them in the Christian life. They kneel in prayer under the coconut trees as they ask God to save the boys and girls scattered about their many islands.

The Mahan paper-shell pecan tree is now the largest tree in the Overholtzer yard, standing proud and tall in its center spot on the front lawn. Symbolic of the life of the indomitable Mr. O, it came through against all odds and now spreads its branches far outward and heavenward — outward in blessing to those it shelters, heavenward in praise to God.

Happy neighborhood children play in the shadow of its grace and beauty.

More of them arrived today, and still more will be coming tomorrow. Like a ragtail army they will soon be poking into odd places and shrieking in delight over the merest trifle. They are the same in any language, nationality or culture, the lovable immortal souls of children. Eagerly they run to the Saviour when they are told of His love for them. Eagerly they pray and "do the work of an evangelist" when light floods their souls.

The ministry begun by the Lord in the heart of Jesse Irvin Overholtzer more than a generation ago continues to grow. Statistics for a recent year show more than 1,800,000 children reached worldwide.

In this particular year in the U.S. alone more than 250,000 received Christ as Saviour in Good News Clubs, open-air evangelism, summer 5-Day Clubs and camps and in special ministries in fairs, hospitals and detention homes.

Teachers, hostesses and helpers numbered more than 28,000. Children's missionary offerings totaled more than $87,000.

Child Evangelism Fellowship is believed to be the largest single agency with an evangelistic outreach exclusively to children.

The great life and work of its founder goes on — capturing the children of this generation for Christ through the heirs of his vision. They have felt the Saviour's heart throb as He said to His disciples, "It is not the will of your Father which is in heaven, that one of these little ones should perish."

Following is the message God used to stir people in North and South America to evangelize children . . .

Child Evangelism as Taught in the Word of God

By J. Irvin Overholtzer

Matthew 18:1-14 is the outstanding Scripture of the whole Bible on the subject of children. If child evangelism is taught in the Bible, we would expect to find it taught here. If the Bible does not teach child evangelism, I do not want anything to do with it. If the Bible *does* teach child evangelism, we should all believe in it and practice it.

What called forth this discourse on children was a question of the disciples. They came asking Jesus who should be the greatest in the Kingdom (Matt. 18:1). In other words, they wanted to know who among believers would get the greatest reward. This was a very proper question. You will find Jesus' answer in these fourteen verses. The Scriptures uniformly teach that the greatest rewards God has to offer will be given to those who win souls (Prov. 11:30; Dan. 12:3). Since this is the case, you would expect our Lord, if He were to answer this question, to deal with soul-winning so that His answer would harmonize with the rest of Scripture.

He *did* deal with soul-winning — the soul-winning of little children! Any attempt to interpret this Scripture which fails to see this fact will miss its real meaning.

Before Jesus uttered a word, He called a little child and set him in the midst of the disciples. Then He used this child as an object lesson. Everything He said in these verses He said about that child or children like that one. Since this is true, it is all important to know how old this child was.

Matthew says the child was little — not an infant; this was not the time He took infants in His arms and blessed them (Luke 18:15-17). This child was a little child, but not an infant. Mark 9:36 throws a flood of light on the question of the age of this child, for that Scripture says Jesus took the child in His arms — not on His lap but in His arms. It is not natural for a man to take a child in his arms unless the child is quite young. This child was probably six or seven or eight years of age, or even younger; certainly not over ten. It was of that age children that Jesus was speaking in these verses (Matt. 18:2).

Even an adult must become childlike to enter the Kingdom

A little child is humble and teachable and trustful. Each of these characteristics is essential to coming to God as lost sinners and accepting salvation by grace — a free gift. Adults have lost these essentials. Only through the agony of repentance and by the grace of God can they acquire them. Since little children already possess these characteristics, Jesus is teaching that it is easier for a child to come to Christ than it is for an adult.

Experience proves this to be so. Children come to Christ readily when given an opportunity to do so (Matt. 18:3).

Many feel it beneath their dignity to be known as "children's workers."

To evangelize children does not bring recognition — they are still children after they accept Christ. They do not add to the strength of the church at once — they do not make paying members.

But Jesus taught that those who would be greatest in God's sight must place the proper estimate on the value of the soul of a little child and act accordingly. He taught that this shows true humility (Matt. 18:4).

Jesus said that to receive one such little child in His name (on a spiritual basis) is as though we received Christ Himself. Mark 9:37 makes this statement even stronger. To receive a little child is as though we received God the Father.

Why does our Lord put such a high value on a little child? The answer is simple. Each little child has an immortal soul. He will spend eternity somewhere. If he grows up in sin and does not come to Christ in his lifetime, he will not spend eternity in Heaven.

To bring souls to Christ is the greatest work in the world. To bring *children* to Christ is just as great a work as bringing adults to Christ.

Many doubt whether little children of six or eight or ten years can believe on Christ and be regenerated by the Holy Spirit. Jesus settled that question forever. He spoke of "Whoso shall offend one of these little ones which believe in me" (Matt. 18:6). John 1:12 gives the promise: "As many as received him, to them gave he power to become the sons of God." There is no age limit here! A little child can qualify and claim it. Is it reasonable to believe that a child of, say, eight years of age can come to Christ and savingly believe?

Does a child of eight sin knowingly? When he sins, is he conscious of guilt? Does a child of that age have intelligence enough to understand the simple Gospel of Christ dying to save sinners? Can such a child make a decision of his own free choice? When these questions are answered, and there is only one way to answer them, it becomes so clear that of course little children can savingly believe. And when they do believe will not God regenerate them according to His promise? Many of our choicest believers — laymen, ministers, and missionaries — testify that they were truly born again when they were little children, some of them even younger than six years of age.

Do little children need salvation?

Our Lord answered this question also, for it is all important. He startles us by saying in the eleventh verse — and remember He was still talking about little children — that He came "to save that which was lost." Are little children lost? Yes, potentially. In verse fourteen He says that it is not the Father's will that they perish, making it very clear that they will perish if they are not brought to Christ. If we will believe what the Word of God says here, we can never rest until we see our children and the children for whom we are responsible savingly converted.

Jesus does not tell us at just what age a certain child will become lost (for all believe that the salvation of infants is secure in the work of Christ on the cross), but that each one of them does pass that unseen line is a self-evident fact. Any given child is potentially lost if he is not brought to Christ as a sinner that the Lord Jesus Christ may save him. Since this is true, the only reasonable and safe thing to do is to lead each child to Christ as early as possible. As soon as a child knows the difference between right and wrong, as soon as he shows evidence of a guilty conscience when he does wrong, he is old enough to have explained to him how God loves him and how Jesus died for his sins. He is old enough to have explained to him how God, in His Word, promises that He will forgive all our sins and that the Lord Jesus will come into our hearts to live if we accept Him as our own Saviour (Matt. 18:11, 14).

Little children can savingly believe, and our Lord made it our duty as believers to bring them to Christ for salvation. Many who have believed in child conversion insist that we must make no effort to bring the child to Christ, that the Holy Spirit must deal with him until he comes to Christ by himself, or comes to us seeking to be led to Christ. Jesus shattered these false theories which have been responsible for the fact that hosts of children have not come to Christ. They could have been led to Him if we had done our duty instead of putting the whole responsibility upon the Holy Spirit and the child.

In verses twelve and thirteen, Jesus gives us the parable of the lost sheep. In these verses He makes it the duty of His disciples to go out and find the lost and bring them into the fold, just as a faithful shepherd would do if a single sheep had gone astray. How ridiculous this parable makes the idea that little children should come to Christ by themselves, for how could a lost sheep come back to the fold by himself without the help of the shepherd? The shepherd, in this parable, is not the Holy Spirit or our Lord, but the disciple. And since Jesus gave this teaching to all of His disciples, the responsibility to evangelize little children rests upon all believers. Remember, He is still dealing with the question of the greatest reward. No one will get the greatest reward who neglects this solemn duty.

Christian parents should evangelize their children

In Ephesians 6:4 believing fathers are commanded to bring up their children in the nurture of the Lord. No father can obey this command without evangelizing his own children. It is the plan of God that the children of believers shall be led to Christ in the home by their own parents. At what age? When they are young enough that they can still be held in the arms. If they were so led, few children of Christian parents would grow up unsaved, and we would go to Heaven by families. This Scripture presupposes that a believing father knows how to lead his child to Christ. Every parent fails in his duty to his children if he does not have that knowledge. God will hold parents responsible for the salvation of their children.

The Church and the Sunday school should evangelize their children

In John 21:15 Jesus commanded Peter to feed His (Jesus') lambs, and beyond question Jesus meant the little children. He was not speaking to Peter as a father but as an apostle or a leader in the church. Here our Lord was making the leaders of the church responsible for the children of the church. They cannot be fed unless they are evangelized. To try to feed unsaved lambs — unsaved children — is not God's plan and it leads to failure. I Corinthians 2:14 tells that unsaved cannot understand spiritual things. Children who go to Sunday school for years but are not born again can only get the "letter" of the Word; but "the letter killeth" (II Cor. 3:6). And how many of our children have been "killed" instead of saved! Is it any wonder that eighty-five per cent of the children leave the Sunday school in the teen ages and most of them never come back? Why? We have killed their interest in and love for the Word of God. They have never seen the beauty of its deeper, spiritual meaning.

So just as it is the duty of believing parents to evangelize their children, our Lord has made it the duty of church leaders to evangelize the children of the Sunday school, and surely this evangelization is to extend to the children in the homes of the whole congregation. At what age should these children be led to Christ? When they are young enough for a man to hold them in his arms. If they were so led, few children of the Sunday school would grow up unsaved. As conditions are at present, millions of those in Sunday school leave it unsaved. I believe God will hold the leaders of the church and Sunday school responsible for the salvation of every child under their care.

All Christians should evangelize unreached children

But the parable of the lost sheep is not dealing with the child in a Christian home or in a Sunday school; rather the straying, the unreached children. Our Lord made all His disciples responsible for the evangelization of these and the only way to reach them is to go out — go out — go out where they are, by every possible means. According to this parable, our Lord's plan for these straying children is to evangelize them first, right where we find them, and then, as it becomes possible, bring them into the fold of the church and the Sunday school. You see God has a threefold plan for the evangelization of little children: in the home, in the church or Sunday school, and then in any place where they can be contacted or gathered. The teaching of the parable is that a shepherd's first duty is to the straying sheep. Our first duty, as believers, is to get the children saved while they are still children, while they are so easy to contact and to evangelize, "while the evil days come not" (Eccles. 12:1) when they are so hard to contact or to win.

Danger of neglecting evangelization of little children

Jesus said, "Take heed that ye despise not [undervalue or neglect] one of these little ones" (Matt. 18:10). The whole tendency with many is to neglect to lead little children to Christ — to put it off until they are older, or to wait for others to do it. Our Lord said little children are not "despised" in Heaven. Heaven is concerned about them. Heaven knows when a little child believes; knows if a certain child is born again or not and, wonderful truth, Heaven assigns a guardian angel to each saved child.

It should be noted that the children referred to in verse ten are the ones mentioned in verse six, the ones "which believe in me." These are the ones who are given guardian angels. If Jesus is so concerned about evangelizing little children, and Heaven is moved by the event of a child's conversion, then why do God's people so neglect this work? Is it not the influence of Satan that causes this? Does not Satan know that little children can be saved, and would he not do everything in his power to have us delay winning them? Does he not know how hard it is to win them when they grow older? Luke 15:10 says, ". . . there is joy in the presence of the angels of God over one sinner that repenteth." Would that not be just as true if the sinner were only a six- or eight-year-old sinner?

Will saved children "hold out"?

So many hesitate to win children to Christ for fear that they will not "hold out." Let us remember that Heaven is guarding every one of them, that each one has an angel of his very own. Experience proves that little children as a group "hold out" better than do adults as a group. Where children do not "live the life" it is usually because they are not born again or because they have been offended by those who should have cared for them. So many children have been led to make a decision on the ground of works instead of grace, and of course they were not born again, so how could they live the life? Every child should have the way of salvation "by grace, through faith" (Eph. 2:8-10) explained to him before he is led to a decision. If this is done carefully and simply, real regeneration will usually follow.

The terrible sin of offending little children

Matthew 18:6 says of those who offend little children that it were better if they were drowned in the depth of the sea. Verses seven to nine say that if those who offend little children had their just deserts, hell fire would be their lot. Why is it such a terrible sin to offend little children regarding spiritual things? — (1) because their eternal welfare is at stake; (2) because they are unable to find the truth by themselves — they are dependent upon us; (3) because if we make no effort to lead them to Christ they naturally think that they cannot come — that they are too young; (4) because little children are eager to please God and to love Jesus if they are told in the right way. They are willing to come to Jesus if someone will lovingly show them how. Their failure to come is our fault and not theirs.

Offending saved children

But, strictly speaking, the teaching in Matthew 18:6 in regard to offending little children has to do with offending little children who already savingly believe. How can this be done and why is it such a terrible sin?

1. When a child accepts Christ in an environment in which those who ought to encourage him to believe that he is saved, doubt and question the conversion of children and naturally question *his* conversion, he, of course, hears that others, perhaps even the deacon or the elder, do not think he is really saved. Unless he has special help from someone, he is likely to begin to doubt that he is a Christian and make no effort to live the life.

Every child who accepts Christ and gives any evidence at all that he is a true believer should have the help and encouragement of all true believers.

2. All those who are born again are "babes" in Christ and should be fed on the milk of the Word (I Pet. 2:2). A little child who is born again is a babe in Christ and still a little child. He must be fed and he does not have knowledge enough to find the "milk" in the Word and feed himself. It is the duty of the adult believers who have him under their care to sort out the milk and feed it to him. If they do not, how can he grow in grace, and whose fault is it when he fails? If we do not feed our children in our homes physically, they will starve and we will soon be in jail. Jesus says that if we fail to care for and feed the children under our care spiritual food, it were better that we were drowned in the depth of the sea. If all of the believers who are guilty of this sin were drowned today, there would be a mighty splash and vacancies in strange places!

3. The reasons it is such a terrible sin to offend believing children are: first, it destroys their faith and Christian life; second, it brings child evangelism into disrepute because of the failure of children who *are* saved to live the life. This failure discourages children's workers and keeps them from doing their duty with the result that millions of children have not been led to Christ who would have gladly come. Hosts of these will never be saved because of our failure. It is easy to see why the sin of offending believing children is so terrible in the sight of God. God grant that it may become terrible in our sight as well!

God has declared His will regarding the salvation of every little child

Jesus summed up His wonderful message on child evangelism and true greatness by brushing aside every doubt as to God's will regarding the salvation of little children. He said it is "not the will of your Father which is in heaven, that one of these little ones should perish" (Matt. 18:14). With these words of our Lord ringing in our ears we can and should go out to win children to Christ everywhere. My experience during many years in child evangelism has been that God is always ready to bless every true effort to evangelize little children, and that the Holy Spirit will instantly regenerate each one who truly believes on the ground of grace.